Annalisa Fineschi – Stefano Filipponi

Texts adapted by Rosaria Punzi

FLORENCE
FOR KIDS

Illustrations by Filippo Sassoli

PLACES IN FLORENCE ON OUR TRIP:

With the patronage of
Florence Municipality

With the patronage of
Istituto degli Innocenti

Lapis Series, graphics and editing by Lapis-snc
via Francesco Ferrara 50, 00191 Roma
tel/fax: +39.06.3295935
e-mail: parisia@mclink.it

Research and scientific advising: Annalisa Fineschi, Stefano Filipponi
Texts adaptation: Rosaria Punzi
General advisor: Carlo Sisi, director of the Pitti Palace Modern Gallery
Translation: Isobel Butters Caleffi
The drawings of the four symbols at the top of page 7 and throughout the book are by Lorenzo Terranera

We wish to thank Stefano Filipponi and Marco Perrone Capano for the photos. The picture on page 81 was created by FACE TO FACE STUDIO for MEMORIE DI ARCHITETTURA who kindly gave permission for it to be published.
Permission to publish the works on pp. 87,90, 97, 103, 105,106,108,110-115, 117, 121-123 has been granted by the Ministry for Arts and the Environment; any other form of reproduction or duplication is forbidden.
We thank the Assessore al Decentramento for research and information, as well as all the other people who have contributed to the making of this book.

ISBN 88-7621-922-6

PREFACE

Dear Children,

When you are looking at a picture or a photo in a book, or perhaps a statue in a square, with a crowd of tourists admiring it, do you ever wonder who the important person is, what they did and why they are portrayed and remembered? Perhaps you even ask the grown ups but they don't know the answer or they give you a long boring answer that doesn't satisfy you at all. How many of you, walking the streets of the city, have found themselves in front of a building, a square or a garden where perhaps you have stopped to play, or wandered inquisitively into a courtyard and have by chance discovered a painting or a fresco without knowing anything about the building, the square, the garden or the fresco: its name, when it was built, or painted or by whom? Yet these places or things struck you because they were so beautiful, and for no particular reason. It's difficult to explain beauty, but you admire it and it captivates you.

We can come to understand it better and to learn the story that lies behind the thousands of beautiful and original things that make Florence so unique. This book can help you find an answer to your questions. It can help you to understand the city better, why so many people come to visit it, and why your parents or schools have brought you to see the squares, museums and churches of Florence.

Discovering Florence is really a never-ending adventure. It could last your whole life and even a bit longer. There are people who have dedicated their whole existence to studying its buildings, works of art, streets and squares. Their hard work means that we can walk around with a better understanding, knowing why it is the way it is today and how it was conceived. Florence, like any city, is above all the result of lots of ideas thought up by many people who, year after year, century after century, have given it a certain look then altered that look, have said, written and done things that have helped to change the way it is lived in and perceived; for example, Masaccio's frescoes in the Brancacci Chapel, the corridor designed by Vasari between the Pitti Palace and Palazzo Vecchio, or bigger works like the Ponte Vecchio, which has resisted the force of the river Arno since the fourteenth century, Brunelleschi's dome or Giotto's Bell Tower - in reality started by Giotto but finished by Pisano and Talenti - as we will learn later on. Then there are things that are not directly visible, that are neither paintings, statues or buildings, such as Dante's poetry, Brunelleschi's theories about perspective, Girolamo Savonarola, Lorenzo de' Medici or Giordano Bruno's political ideas.

When you have finished reading this book and learnt to answer the questions it asks; when you have discovered the history that lies behind the stones, colours, walls and open spaces of the city, you will most definitely know more than grown ups know.

You children, who come from distant countries, or who might even be born here will be the ones to change Florence after us, so it is you who need to know about the city and what lies hidden behind the present so that it can have a future that keeps its link with such an important past.

The mayor
Mario Primicerio

EQUIPMENT FOR TOURISTS

Rucksack containing:
- snack
- drinking cup
- light waterproof
  (in winter)
- sun hat
  (in summer)
- notepad pen
- camera with
  film
- this guide book

HOW TO READ THE GUIDE BOOK

CHRONOLOGICAL TABLE

1300

1400

On pages 10 and 11, there are two tables to help you find your way through the different historical periods. The colour scale shows the earliest periods in purple and goes through the various colours until it gets to the most recent ones in red. You won't find the exact dates but you will have an idea of the succession of events and of how long each historical period lasted.

STYLES

Following the routes you will often read about the variety of manners, techniques and materials used through the centuries in the different fields of art (sculpture, architecture, painting) by great artists who left very strong marks on the city. You will find these explained in a way that is easy to understand under the general heading of styles on page 12.

MAPS

At the beginning of each itinerary you will find a map that will help you to find your way along the route. Try to follow it, to know where you are all the time and in which direction you need to go.

SYMBOLS

 the text tells a story

 the text descri-bes the interior of a building

 the text describes the exterior of a building

The routes are explained in a coloured box and a sign like this. Always read the explanations consulting the map at the beginning of each itinerary.

The @ symbol means that the subject has already been dealt with more fully on the page indicated by the number that follows this symbol. So if you are interested you can always find out more by turning to the page.

DATES

When we talk about centuries we generally use Roman numerals. For instance XII century is read twelfth century and it means the period from 1100 to the year 1199. In fact the first century after Christ goes from the year 0 to 99, the second from 100 to 199 and so on.

A FEW IMPORTANT TIPS

Get together with a friend, the trip will be more memorable and you can compare and discuss what you see.

On your trips around town always try to discover new and interesting things.

Take notes and photos; don't only photograph build-ings but your friends too, it will be more fun look-ing at them later.

Florence's museums are often crowded. If you don't want to get stuck in long queues try to go when they open or at lunch time. The best time to visit is between November and February, the "worst" between April and June.

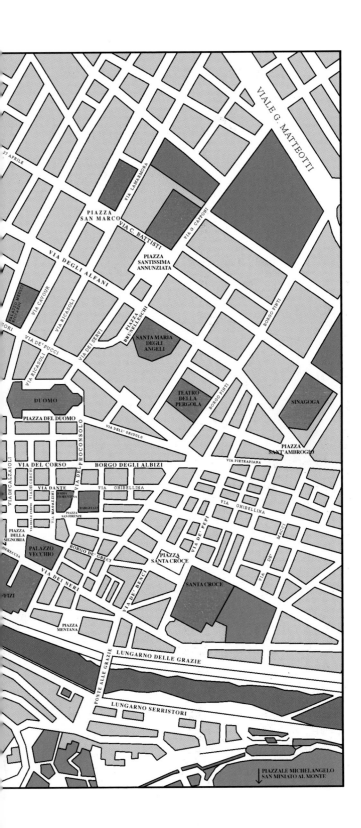

3000 B.C.	Early occupation of the area
1000 B.C.	Settlement of Apennine peoples
700 B.C.	The Etruscans settled in Tuscany
	The Romans founded *Florentia*
Anno 0	Birth of Jesus Christ
100 A.D.	
200 A.D.	Martyrdom of St. Miniato
300 A.D.	
400 A.D.	Siege of the Ostrogoths
	Fall of the Western Roman Empire
	Barbarian invasions
500 A.D.	
600 A.D.	Lombardic dominion
700 A.D.	
800 A.D.	Dominion of the Franks: Charlemagne
900 A.D.	
1000 A.D.	Florence capital of the Duchy
1100 A.D.	Struggles for investitures between papacy and empire
	Treaty of Worms: end of battles for investitures
	Fiesole razed to the ground by Florence
	Struggles between Federico Barbarossa and the Municipalities
	Peace of Constancy between Municipalities and the Empire
	Struggles in Florence between Guelphs and Ghibellines

1200	Podestà rules the Municipality
	The merchants organise themselves into groups called "Guilds"
	Battle of Montaperti: the Ghibellines come to power
	The Guelphs dominate the city
	The "Priorate" takes power
	Florence is one of Europe's most powerful cities
1300	The white Guelphs are driven from the city
	Period of crisis
	The plague
	Revolt of the Ciompi
	Oligarchy
1400	

	Cosimo the Elder absolute ruler of Florence
	Lorenzo the Magnificent rules the city
	The conspiracy of the Pazzi
	Florence is the major cultural centre of Europe
1500	Expulsion of the Medici. Florence becomes a republic
	The Medici return to the city
	Cosimo I de'Medici becomes first grand duke of Tuscany
1600	
1700	
	End of the Medici dynasty: the Grand Duchy is governed by the Hapsburg Lorraines
	The Uffizi gallery is opened to the public
1800	Florence is annexed to the Napoleonic empire
	The Lorraines return to the city
	The Florentines expel Leopold II of Lorraine
	The Kingdom of Italy is proclaimed
	Florence is made capital of Italy
1900	
	First World War
	Italy is governed by Fascists
	Second World War
	The Italian Republic is proclaimed
	The flood: Florence is submerged by water

ARCHITECTURAL STYLES

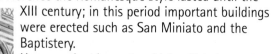

Each artist has his own way of working, but
experts have observed that there are charac-
teristics common to those who lived during
the same period, close to one another. These
similarities make it possible to define the artis-
tic language, or style, of the various eras. By
keeping these common elements in mind you
will be able to recognise the style of the buildings you see as you wander around Florence.
But watch out! It's a little like being a detective, you have to
observe carefully, collect evidence and not be taken in by fakes!

ROMANESQUE

A few decades before the year 1000 the whole of Europe experienced a kind of rebirth: cities began to be governed independently
and the economy flourished; buildings, especially religious ones,
were renewed. In Florence the Romanesque style lasted until the

XIII century; in this period important buildings
were erected such as San Miniato and the
Baptistery.
Here are the elements which will help you to
recognise Romanesque architecture in
Florence:
walls decorated using coloured marble cut into
geometric shapes (especially green and white);
classical architectural elements such as
columns, semicircular arches used to separate
the walls or interior spaces;
the use of very small windows, either square or with semicircular
arches surmounted by a triangular cornice, the tympanum;
walls decorated with mosaics (usually on a golden background) and
intarsia (a mosaic is made up of small pieces that are all the same
size, while intarsia has bigger pieces and dif-
ferent shapes).

GOTHIC

The word "gothic" was used as an insult (the Goths
were barbarians) to indicate a style that originated
in France in the XII century and then spread throughout Europe,
where it remained until the beginning of the fifteenth century. By
applying the rules of the Gothic style, bigger churches could be
built and decorated and new types of buildings put up. These, for
instance the Bargello and Palazzo Vecchio, both seats of government, answered to the needs of the politics and expanding economy of the cities.

In order to get the results they wanted, architects replaced the old elements used in the Romanesque period and introduced others, for instance:
pointed or ogive arches which enabled buildings to be made higher because they could support more weight.

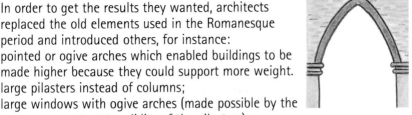

large pilasters instead of columns;
large windows with ogive arches (made possible by the

solidity of the pilasters);
decorations using coloured marbles and sculptures that were richer and more intricate than the Romanesque ones;
painted decorations on walls or on wood instead of mosaics.

RENAISSANCE

Renaissance means rebirth and it was the name given to the period in which all fields of culture experienced a return to the models of beauty and harmony established in classical art.

The period went roughly from the fifteenth century to the sixteenth.
During the Middle Ages religion had been the pivot around which life and culture revolved.
In the Renaissance the centre of attention became man, his abilities, his desire to know and experiment in all fields. It was an age of great artists and also one where new worlds were being discovered. The artists' patrons changed too. It was no

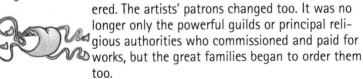

longer only the powerful guilds or principal religious authorities who commissioned and paid for works, but the great families began to order them too.

Important noble palaces were built. These stood alone, isolated from the rest of the city, so that their owners could show off their full wealth to everyone; even religious buildings now were being paid for by rich families, who placed their coat of arms in full view. The style of this period is not characterised by rich decoration or size, but by the ordered subdivision of space, harmony and convenience.

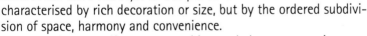

Here are some hints to help you recognise Renaissance architecture:
a return to the use of classical elements (pointed arches, columns instead of pilasters, tympana, domes);
subdivision of the buildings according to regular, repeated patterns;
white plastered walls alternating with grey stone parts (doors, windows, arches, columns);
decoration limited to certain areas.

1.   Ponte Vecchio
2.   Piazza della Signoria
3.   Loggia dei Lanzi
4.   Badia Fiorentina
5.   Palazzo del Bargello
6.   Orsanmichele
7.   Piazza della Repubblica
8.   Palazzo Strozzi
9.   Palazzo Davanzati
10.   Loggia del Mercato Nuovo

MEDIEVAL FLORENCE
PLACES OF GOVERNMENT
AND COMMERCE

Palazzo Vecchio: weekdays 9-19, holidays 8-13;
(closed Thursdays)

Badia Fiorentina: 9-11.45, 16.30-18;

Orsanmichele: 9-12, 16-18;
(closed first and last Monday of every month)

FLORENCE IN ANCIENT TIMES

Recent excavation work carried out in the centre of Florence has shown that by 3000 B.C. Italian tribes had already settled in the area. Here the valley of the river Arno , which flows into the Tyrrheanian Sea, meets that of the river Mugnone, which descends from the Appenines. These natural passages were easily travelled even in ancient times. Furthermore, just at this point the Arno becomes narrower, making it easier to cross. Consequently, the area was strategic for human traffic and goods, and it continued to be inhabited though the centuries that followed.

When the Etruscans (already powerful in this region) decided to create a new city in the fifth century B.C., they did not choose the plain on which Florence stood , but a nearby hill. Fiesole was born and it was from here that the Etruscans were able to dominate the area between the VI and II centuries B.C. But in the I century B.C. the Romans defeated the Etruscans as part of their gradual conquest of Italy. They subdued Fiesole and seized control of all its territories.

According to legend it was some of Julius Caesar's veterans (retired soldiers) who founded the city of Florentia in 59 B.C., in spring or, as the Romans said, in the period of the ludi florales (games held in honour of the goddess Flora) from which the name is said to derive.

According to recent studies, in actual fact the new city was built later, during the reign of Augustus (27 B.C.-14 A.D.) and the name Florentia was intended as a desire for prosperity. Roman Florence was a quadrilateral, it was protected by city walls and divided internally by a regular network of streets and blocks. This layout can still be seen in the centre of the city.

To cross the Arno the Etruscans had organised a service of ferry boats; the Romans instead built the first of Florence's bridges, not far from where the Ponte Vecchio is now. The Roman city's maximum splendour was during the reign of emperor Hadrian (117-138 A.D.). Then there were about 10.000 inhabitants, it had a river port, an amphitheatre, a theatre and large thermal baths!

When the power of the Romans began its decline, this generalised decadence was felt in Florence too and large numbers of the popu-lation abandoned the city and the barbarian invasions... did the rest.

MEDIEVAL FLORENCE: THE FREE COMUNE

After the barbarian invasions, Florence's population was reduced to under 5.000 inhabi-tats.
The old buildings were aban-doned and the townspeople took refuge in the religious centres that had arisen around the city.

In 774, Charlemagne conquered central-northern Italy and brought a certain amount of peace and prosperity to the region, but he chose Lucca as the capital of the duchy of Tuscany.

Then, little by little, Florence began to grow and become repopulat-ed and the marquises that governed the duchy decided to move its capital there. In the years that followed the city took the side of the marchioness of Tuscany, Matilde of Canossa, who fought with the pope against the emperor. Matilde, grateful to the city for its help, granted a great many privileges and in 1078 had new walls built around the city. When she died in 1115, neither the emperor nor the papacy were able to control the grand duchy of Tuscany any longer.

The region's cities began to govern by themselves, becoming the Free Comunes.

During the XII century Florence started to fight against the nearby towns so as to extend its territories and become more and more powerful. The first victim was its rival Fiesole which was defeated in 1125. Florence had by then become the richest and most highly populated town in the region.

Its government was in the hands of a few powerful families who competed for control. The fights were so bloody that the nobles grouped together in associations of friendly families called consorterie and built towers which linked up with one another, creating lots of small fortifications inside the city.

So as to get a bit of peace it was decided to place the governing of the city in the hands of the "Podestà", a noble and wealthy foreigner who did not belong to any of the Florentine families.

However, the fighting did not stop all the same, and the rival families joined together in the Guelphs, who supported the pope and the Ghibellines who supported the emperor. The artisans and merchants

could not work properly under these conditions and decided to form an association called "the People" and, in 1250, chose a Captain of the People to govern beside the Podestà. But not even this was enough and in 1282 power was placed in the hands of Priors elected by the various Guilds. The Guilds were associations of people who did the same job and together they regulated their own commercial activity.

Consequently, the nobility was gradually removed from power as it did not belong to any Guild.

Despite the continuous fighting, the city prospered: artisans produced widely consumed goods that merchants sold to the East and the West; the Florentine banks were rich and their money, the gold Florin, was the only coin accepted all over Europe. Much of the wealth accumulated was used to embellish Florence with the work of famous artists, such as Giotto (1267-1337) and Arnolfo di Cambio (1245-1302). Large public buildings were constructed such as the Bargello and Palazzo Vecchio, roads and squares were improved, new bridges built and the cathedral - then the biggest church in the world - was begun. New city walls, so large they did not need to be extended until the nineteenth century, also belong to the same period.

However the political situation did not improve. The Guelphs, who had definitively defeated the Ghibellines, separated into the 'blacks' and the 'whites'. In 1302 the black Guelphs, aided by the pope, chased all the whites from Florence. Even Dante Alighieri, the poet, was forced to leave his city.

In spite of all the internal conflict at the beginning of the 14th century Florence was one of the most famous and richest cities in the world. It had to face enormous problems however: the flood of 1333, insolvency of the banks and mercantile companies and the plague of 1348.

The government of the Priors turned out to be incapable of handling such a difficult situation, made more difficult by the divisions between the major Guilds (the ones which earned the most money) and the minor Guilds. Power had been taken from the nobility in the hope of peace but it never came about.
In 1382 the Florentines decided that the city should be governed by a restricted group of families.

PONTE VECCHIO

The Ponte Vecchio is the oldest of Florence's bridges. It was built at a point where the Arno narrows, making it much easier to cross.

The river destroyed the bridge many times and each time it was rebuilt more solidly. In 1345 it was made so wide and so strong that it has resisted up to the present.

Where today there are jewellers' shops, in the Middle Ages the bridge was teeming with greengrocers', butchers', fishmongers' and craftsmen's shops. It must have been very busy, with lots of toing and froing, cries from the vendors, shoppers chat and the noise of the cartwheels.

Try to imagine the bridge full of people buying and selling and shouting. Bits of lettuce or fennel and oranges strewn on the ground. Then the smell: just think that the tanners used to put their hides to soak in horse urine and the shopkeepers used to throw their refuse into the river. It was dirty and smelly, but it was certainly full of life.

CORRIDOIO VASARIANO

However, as you can imagine, this did not at all suit the Medici, who to get from their residence at the Pitti Palace to Palazzo Vecchio, had to pass through an area so unfitting to their station; an area, what is more, where they were an easy target for ambushes. In 1565 duke Cosimo I called architect Giorgio Vasari (1511-1574) to solve the problem for him.

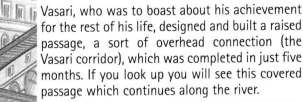

Vasari, who was to boast about his achievement for the rest of his life, designed and built a raised passage, a sort of overhead connection (the Vasari corridor), which was completed in just five months. If you look up you will see this covered passage which continues along the river.

In 1593, to make the area a little less dirty and untidy, grand duke Ferdinando I expelled all the merchants and craftsmen, replacing them with goldsmiths and jewellers from whom he could ask a much higher rent!

Walk along via Por Santa Maria now. On the left of the street a short way along you will see the tower where the Amidei lived: a safe but uncomfortable refuge in case of attacks from the enemy.

On the façade look for the detail shown in the drawing: these are the bridge holes, used to support the wooden poles on which the projections rested. These projections were temporary structures that stuck out of the outer walls and they were used for moving from one tower to another without having to go down to the ground. The sentries used them and they were very useful for throwing arrows and boiling oil down on top of any enemy who tried to take possession of the building. The other constructions in the area were destroyed during the Second World War, but in the Middle Ages this side of the street was entirely occupied by the many towers of the Amidei faction.

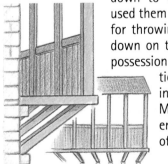

PIAZZA DELLA SIGNORIA

Continuing along via Por Santa Maria you will come to via Vacchereccia on the right. From here you can see piazza della Signoria. Go there.

Now you are in one of the most famous squares in the world . The area was already inhabited in prehistoric times and, during the Roman era when Florentia was founded, many noblemen's houses were built here and, later, large public buildings as well.

In the Middle Ages the square was a small open area in the quarter of the Uberti, the noble family who headed the Ghibellines of Florence. But defeated by the Guelphs, the Ghibellines were exiled, their property confiscated and their houses destroyed. By order of the Comune, no other buildings were to be constructed on the site where the traitors' towers had stood. Instead a large square was created to represent the freedom of the Comune of Florence. It was forbidden to conduct dishonourable business here or to gamble, and carts were not allowed to pass. Fines for those not respecting the regulations were much higher than in the rest of the city.

PALAZZO VECCHIO OR DELLA SIGNORIA

The palace of the Signoria was built at the end of the thirteenth century to house the Priors and Standard-bearers of Justice, who together made up the government of the city: "the Signoria". Since then it has always been the people's square and that of Florence's governors, and its history mirrors that of the city.

When the end of the Republic came (1530), the Medici family, whose dukedom now began, went to live in the palace, making it "Ducal". It was given the name "Vecchio", meaning old, when the Medicis moved to their new residence, the Pitti Palace. In the nineteenth century the parliament of Tuscany moved in and, during the short spell when Florence was capital of Italy, the national parliament. Nowadays it is the seat of the Municipality. Palazzo Vecchio had been erected to defend the Priors and to dominate in size and importance over the many towers built by the nobility. So as to make sure that its tower was the highest in the city, it was established that no private ones were to be over 30 metres high!

The existing towers that were too high had to be lowered.

Go up to the palace and look at the thickness of the outer wall. It is made of strong stone (a material that comes from nearby quarries); the way

it has been worked, with big regular square-shaped blocks that stick out slightly, is called "rustication".

The outer projections, made in stone for the first time here, form a sort of corridor where the sentries would walk.

If you wish you can visit the inside of the palace now, otherwise continue on your way and come back when you have completed the first itinerary dedicated to the Medici.
The moment you go in you will feel that you are in a palatial residence, very different from the outside which looks like a medieval fortress.

Indeed, when Cosimo I de' Medici officially became lord of Florence, he decided to leave his family home and go to live in the palace of the Signoria together with his wife Eleanor of Toldeo. The palace, which since the Middle Ages had been the austere seat of the city governors, was certainly not up to the standards of a family with princely taste, so Cosimo had the old part renewed and installed apartments for his wife there. For himself he built new rooms.

In the first courtyard you can see the decorations carried out in 1565 by a group of artists led by Giorgio Vasari. These were executed to celebrate the marriage of Francesco, Cosimo's son, to Joan of Austria, who was related to the emperor. So as to receive the noble and influential new bride in a befitting manner, Cosimo had the walls frescoed with views of the Austrian cities where the young lady had grown up. He decorated the courtyard with gilt stuccoes and a large

marble fountain, surmounted by a statue by the sculptor Andrea di Cione, called Verrocchio (1435-1488).

Go across the courtyard and up the stairway on the right to the first floor. Go through the door on your right into the imposing **room of the Cinquecento** carried out in 1495 after the expulsion of the Medici from Florence. A new form of government, inspired by friar Girolamo Savonarola, was created at this time designed to give more power to the people. The big room you are in was built to house the new general parliament.

When Cosimo came to live in the palace he decided to renew this room which brought back bad memories for his family. He completely changed the furnishings and turned it into an audience chamber. He took out the benches where the representatives of the people sat and raised the side..... on which his throne stood! Then he he had the whole room decorated with frescoes, paintings and sculptures that recalled the history of Florence and his family.

Look to the left of the entrance at the statues that surrounded the throne: they represent important Medici's: in the centre is Leo I, the first Medici pope, on the left is the commander Giovanni of the Black Bands, father of Cosimo I and on the right Alessandro I, duke before him. Then look at Cosimo I in the centre of the ceiling, with a crown of laurel like the conquerors in antiquity, but also with the crown of grand duke. Around him the coats of arms of the Municipality and the Guilds, now powerless, pay him homage.

The princes of the sixteenth century were not only interested in large official rooms though. Their palaces always had small private rooms too, where they could retire to meditate. These were called "studioli" and were small studies. Go to **Francesco I's studiolo** on the right of the entrance. Here Cosimo's son dedicated himself in peace and tranquillity to his scientific interests, "under the careful eye" of his parents, Cosimo and Eleanor, of whom there are two portraits.

In the wall cupboards that line this "room of wonders", Francesco kept rare and precious items belonging to the worlds of nature and art - coins, stones, pieces of glass.

On the same floor were other richly decorated rooms, each dedicated to the glorification of a different member of the Medici family.

Go towards the floor where the **quarters of the Elements** is. It is made up of a series of rooms, seemingly dedicated to various mythological characters, but whose aim was once again to exalt the Medici!

Every room corresponds perfectly to one on the floor below, so that the room of Hercules is above that of Giovanni of the Black Bands, while that of the mighty Jupiter, king of all the gods is right above Cosimo I's room. Now go to Eleanor of Toledo's rooms.

These belong to the medieval part of the palace that was completely renewed for her.

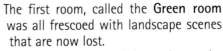

The first room, called the **Green room** was all frescoed with landscape scenes that are now lost.

Very well conserved instead are the decorations in the chapel on the right; these were carried out by Agnolo Bronzino (1503-1572). When the beautiful and powerful wife of Cosimo wished for a moment of reflection or to work she sat at the writing desk you see before you.

From here you can go through the other five rooms that make up **Eleanor's quarters** - they were all frescoed by the Flemish artist Giovanni Stradaro (1523-1605). The subject and decoration of these rooms regard famous women who possessed the same virtues as the duchess.

The room of the Sabine women, who after being captured by the Romans prevented war between them and the women's relatives; the room of Esther from the name of the Biblical queen who agreed to risk her own life to save her people; the room of Penelope, the patient and tenacious wife of Ulysses, and finally the room of Gualdrada, a young Florentine who had had the courage to refuse the kiss of the emperor Otto IV and was rewarded for her sincerity.

When you have been through Eleanor's apartments you will find yourself in a narrow corridor that leads to the **chapel of the Priors**, where these powerful personages would withdraw to meditate and pray.

Next you will come to the **Audience hall** reserved for court hearings and then you will come to the large **room of the Lilies**, so called because of the ceiling decorations.

Here though the lily is not the symbol of Florence, but that of the French Anjou family, influential allies of the Florentine Guelphs.
Compare the two types of flower.

Opposite the entrance is the way to the **room of the geography maps**, where Cosimo kept his most precious works of art and objects in big cupboards painted with all the parts of the world known at the time.

Go out, turn left and go down the stairs to the ground floor. Your visit to the palace is finished. How many rooms have you seen? A lot, of course; yet just think that the Medici left this palace because they found it... too small! When you go to the Pitti palace you will see their magnificent residence.

Now that you are back in the square , look at the fountain near the corner of the palace.

Some say that the huge and ungainly statue of sea god Neptune, known to the Florentines as "il Biancone", the big white one, resembles duke Cosimo I. The duke appears officially however in another statue. He is the one portrayed on horseback in the large monument you see on the left.

Go now and see the statues in front of the palace: some have become symbols of Florence and its power. On the left is the **Marzocco**, a lion with its paw on the coat of arms of the city. Its strange name comes from Mars, god of war and protector of Florence during Roman times. Although it was much loved by the Florentines, this sculpture was rather unlucky. The medieval marzocco was ruined and was replaced by one by Donatello (1386-1466) at the beginning of the fifteenth century. But the statue began to deteriorate and it was moved to the Bargello museum and a copy of it was put in the square.

Still in front of the palace today is a copy of the statue of **Judith and Holofernes**, also by Donatello (the original is nowadays inside Palazzo Vecchio) and the statue which has become the symbol of Florence, Michelangelo's **David** (the original is housed at the Accademia gallery @96).

If the Marzocco represented the strength of the Municipality, the David and Judith recall the cunning with which the Florentine republic managed to keep ahead of its enemies. Both Judith and David defeated adversaries who were far stronger than they: Judith pretended to befriend the general Holofernes, who was laying siege to her city and, while he was sleeping, cut his head off. David instead, killed the mighty giant Goliath by hitting him with a stone from a sling on the forehead, the only spot on his body not protected by armour.

LOGGIA DEI LANZI

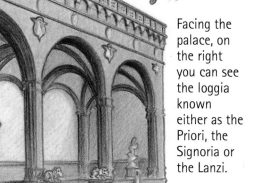

Facing the palace, on the right you can see the loggia known either as the Priori, the Signoria or the Lanzi.

The Priors role was so important that during the two months in which they governed, they were not allowed out of the palace.

They only appeared before the people on important occasions, dressed in their elaborate ceremonial clothes. It was a really special sight to see them. If it rained though the ceremony was held in the nearby church of San Pier Scheraggio and not everyone was able to get in. So it was decided to built a large loggia on the square. A loggia is a covered space enclosed by arcades In 1376 work began and it was completed in just six years. From that moment on the loggia dei Priori was used for all the most important ceremonies held in Florence.

When the Republic ended in 1530, the loggia's original function was lost and it was used by the Lansquenets, German mercenaries in the service of the Medici. This building, conceived as a symbol of the Republic, ended up by having the name of its most hated enemy.

The loggia was then turned into an open air museum with ancient Greek and Roman statues as well as modern, i.e. Renaissance, ones.

Either side of the central staircase you can see two lions. They look the same, but actually the one on the right is Roman, while the other was sculpted in the sixteenth century. In the arcade on the right hand side of the loggia you can see the **Rape of the Sabine** women, a very curious statue created almost as a bet.

In 1580 a Flemish artist named Jean de Boulogne (1529-1608), known as Giambologna, was working at the Medici court . His contemporaries however did not think much of his work and some had even gone so far as to say that he was incapable of sculpting a body in movement.

In answer to this, Giambologna took a huge block of marble, already roughly hewn and seemingly unusable and created an interlacing of bodies in the most complicated positions possible and called it the Rape of the Sabines.

You can also see the sculpture of **Menelaus** holding the dead body of his friend Patroclus. It is a Roman statue but it is a copy of a more ancient Greek one.

The statues of women that you see on the wall behind are also very old. They were brought here from Rome in 1780.

From piazza della Signoria go along via delle Farine (the small street on the left looking at the statue of Cosimo on horseback) and continue as far as the crossroads and via della Condotta.

Nowadays these streets are full of people, but they were even more animated in the four-teenth century - stalls exhibiting their wares stood outside all the shops, horses and mules were 'parked' all over the place, and if you looked up you would have seen the small sus-

pended bridges that connected the various buildings and made the streets dark even during the day.

Go down via dei Cerchi and look for a line inscribed on the wall on the left. It is the "Florentine arm", 58 centimetres long.

When merchants arrived in town they had to measure their lengths of material against this so as to know how long they were in Floren-tine "bracci" or arms and con-sequently the price at which they were to be sold.

BADIA FIORENTINA

Now go on until you get to the intersection with via Dante Alighieri, then turn right and go along it until you reach the ancient Castagna tower where the first meeting of the Priors' government was held in 1282.

The tower is part of the Floren-tine badia, the oldest monastery in Florence.

It was founded in 978 by the mother of marquis Ugo of Tuscany. Ugo was an important personage in Medieval Florence, much loved by his fellow citizens. Dante called him the 'great baron'. The abbey's monks were rich and powerful but not even they could free themselves from the Municipality's control. Just imagine, in 1307 the Priors deliberately damaged the big bell tower to get payment for a tax. The lives of the people in this whole quarter were however punctuated by the ringing of the bells of the Castagna tower and the abbey's storerooms were so big that the road behind the building is called... via dei Magazzini (Storeroom road).

Go to the entrance on via Dante Alighieri.

Until 1285 it was a one single large space, then Arnolfo di Cambio designed numerous alterations. This famous architect turned it into a church with a cross-shaped ground plan and rebuilt the bell tower, giving it a hexagonal ground plan.

Over the years that followed it underwent various modifications and additions. Even the tomb of Ugo of Tuscany was completely remodelled in the fifteenth century. On the right of the altar is a small door leading to the cloisters of the Aranci. It is decorated with fifteenth century frescoes illustrating scenes from the life of St. Benedict.

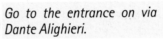

PALAZZO DEL BARGELLO

When you are back in via Dante continue to via del Proconsolo, then turn right. Just ahead you will find yourself at the Bargello palace.

It is the oldest public building in Florence and was built in 1255. Until then the municipal government met either in churches or private buildings that they rented (such as the Castagna tower) but so as to provide hospitality and protection for the Captain of the People it was decided that a new building was needed. The Bargello looks like a fortress and it was so popular that it was used as a model for palazzo Vecchio, although the two buildings are not exactly the same.

Try to find the differences (S = same, D = different)

Shape of the building	S D	Materials used	S D
Position of the tower	S D	Type of projections	S D

Originally the Bargello only had two storeys. It is easy to spot the part added on because the blocks of stone are much smaller than the others and the division is marked by a horizontal strip of stone called a string course.

The palace was used for different things over the years and consequently its name changed too. Originally it was called the Captain of the People's palace, then that of the Podestà, because the Podestà lived there. Bargello was the name given to the Captain of Justice, head of the grand duchy's police. The Captain moved into the palace when it became a prison in 1574. Since the end of the nineteenth century it has been the home of the National Museum (or Bargello Museum @100).

Via del Proconsolo where you are now runs along the site of the old Roman walls. Want to prove it?

One of the wall's lookout towers stood right in front of the site where the Bargello was built. Archaeologists have marked the point where the tower was with a big circle. See if you can find it.

PALACE OF THE GUILD OF JUDGES AND NOTARIES

Walking along via del Proconsolo, on the left looking at the Bargello, you will come to no. 6, the building of the Guilds of Judges and Notaries, the most important of the major Guilds.

This corporation was so influential that its consul was considered head of all the other Guilds and he was called the Proto-consolo or first consul, which is where the name of the street comes from.

PALAZZO DELLA CONGIURA

Just beyond no. 10 you will find the palace of the Pazzi family, also known as the palace of the "Conspiracy" (@66). It was built in the middle of the fifteenth century.

Go left down via del Corso. This is a very old street and is on the site of the decumanus, one of the most important streets of the Roman city. Dante Alighieri lived here at the end of the thirteenth century.

Dante's house

PALAZZO PORTINARI-SALVIATI

At no. 6 via del Corso is the Portinari-Salviati palace. At the beginning of the four-teenth century Folco Portinari lived here. He was father of the young girl whom Dante fell in love with. What was her name?

1. Lucia	2. Francesca	3. Beatrice

... you'll soon find out anyway!

Grandfather dear

DANTE ALIGHIERI

Dante (whose name means he who gives and is the diminutive of Durante meaning he who endures) was born at the end of May in 1265. His parents were Alighiero, a nobleman and a Guelph and Bella his mother. By the age of 12 he had already lost both his parents, so he was brought up by his grandfather Bellincione who allowed him to dedicate himself to his beloved studies.

Before this though, an important event had already marked his life. One fine spring day when he was just nine years old, he met Beatrice Portinari, a beautiful eight year old and he fell in love.

He was not to see her again for 9 years, and when he did she was all dressed in white. This time the young girl greeted him. Dante, mad with happiness returned to his home and decided to write a book

entirely dedicated to telling the story of his love: the New Life.

Sadly, Beatrice died just a few years later when she was only 24 and Dante, who was never to forget her, decided to give her an important role in his great masterpiece, the Divine Comedy, where Beatrice is the guide sent from the sky to lead him to Paradise.

Right from an early age, Dante went to the best schools in the city and was taught by masters who not only transmitted to him a passion for studying but also for politics and the values that lie at the heart of good government.

In 1285 he married Gemma Donati, whom he had been promised to since the age of 12. They were to have three children, Pietro, Jacopo and Antonia and perhaps a Giovanni as well.

When he was 30 he became active in political life as a white Guelph but, being proud and rather lofty, he immediately made a lot of enemies.

His political career was brusquely interrupted after just 7 years because the victory of the black Guelphs forced him into exile.

Off to bed with

It is during these years that he imagines the journey through the three kingdoms (hell, purgatory and paradise) that he describes in his masterpiece: the Comedy (Divine is added later by others). It took him nearly 20 years to write and all of these were spent in exile as he wandered through Verona, Treviso, Lucca and Ravenna.

He died in Ravenna on 13 September 1321 when he was only 56 without ever seeing his beloved Florence again.

DANTE'S HOUSE

The poet's house was near here but it no longer exists. At the beginning of the twentieth century a fake "Dante's house" was built in piazza San Martino. If you would like to go and see it take a left turning, go past the underpass and a little further on you will come to the square. Although it is a reconstruction it will give you an idea about how the real one would have been.

DONATI TOWER

Go back to via del Corso to no. 31 where you can see what remains of the tower of the Donati, the powerful family that forced Dante to flee his city.

It is true that the great poet found love close to home, but he found his most dangerous enemies equally close. It was the Donati, leaders of the black faction who, during a fight between the rival families, started a fire that in 1304 destroyed over 1000 buildings in the city! These included the corn market, which was to have an unusual future; although it was rebuilt, it ended up by becoming a church.

To find it, go along via del Corso to the crossroads with via del Calzaioli, turn left and you will soon be at the Orsanmichele church.

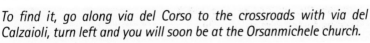

ORSANMICHELE

The church has a long history which explains its unusual name. In 750 A.D. a small oratory was built in the vegetable garden of a monastery dedicated to St. Michael. Because of this the church was called San Michele in Orto (St. Michael's in the Vegetable garden), then shortened to Orsanmichele.

Many years later, in 1240, during Florence's period of great development, the Municipality had the oratory demolished to make way for a big open market. It was always very crowded because, apart from the merchants selling their corn and cereals, there was also a Madonna who was considered to perform miracles. So in 1290, Arnolfo di Cambio was commissioned to design a loggia to shelter her on rainy days.

This loggia-market was destroyed in the great fire of 1304 and it was entirely rebuilt with two floors added for storeroom space. In the meantime, in 1359 Andrea di Cione, known as Orcagna, constructed a tabernacle to protect the painting that had replaced the image of the miracle-working Madonna of the early loggia. (A tabernacle is a closed niche containing consecrated bread known as the Host, or holy pictures).

However, something unexpected happened: perhaps because of the memory of the old picture or because of the beauty of the new tabernacle, the loggia began to be frequented by an increasing number of the faithful, to the extent that at the end of the four-teenth century it was decided to move the market, enclose the loggia and turn the building into a church. Since it stood in the merchants' quarter, the Guilds decided to cover the cost of decorating it, painting the interior and placing sculptures on the exterior.

On each external pilaster there is a different statue depicting the protector saint of each Guild. These were all sculpted by the great artists of the time and their beauty was to express the power of those who had paid for them. The coat of arms of each guild appears beside its statue.

Try recognising statues and coats of arms by solving these riddles

1. Saints with books and beards there are a few
but the one you want has a winged lion beneath him
and the coat of arms of he who works with wool and sells old things.

2. I could say that this saint has a slender cross,
or that he has a cloak but it would certainly be more help to
know that at his feet two eagles grip a bale of cloth in their claws

3. Four are the saints, and that's enough to find them
but you must guess what the men below are doing
and whose Guild has a tool of its trade as its symbol.

4. To end find the saint who as a bishop is dressed
but who at the bottom you see clothed as a craftsman
shoeing a horse by the devil obsessed.

Enter the church in via dell'Arte della Lana (opposite via dei Calzaioli). Its strange shape reminds us that it was once a market.

Look for other signs of its original use:

1. the stairs that led to the storerooms upstairs

2. an odd-looking container with
handles: it is a bushel and was used for
measuring corn. By counting the
number of sacks, all containing the
same quantities, is was easy to
know how much corn there was in
the stores.

3. The openings in two of the pilasters where the stored
corn was sent down chutes to the ground floor.

Even after the market had become a church the area
continued to be used for commerce. Around here were
the main markets and the seats of many of the Guilds.
The narrow lanes were always crowded with vendors and
buyers.

Nowadays it is hard to imagine all this because during the nineteenth century the area was cleaned up and the tiny streets and old
buildings were replaced by wide roads and large new buildings.

PALAZZO DELL'ARTE DELLA LANA

However not everything disappeared. When you come out of the
church you will see the Wool Guild build-
ing. It was the home of one of the wealthiest guilds in the city. At the end of the
thirteenth century there were over 200
shops and some 30.000 workers who
belonged to it. They produced 100.000
lengths of material each year, about a
tenth of the whole European market! Walk
round the building then turn right down
via Calimala (whose name perhaps comes
from calle maior meaning Main street).
The cloth sellers shops were here and this
is why their powerful corporation was
known as the Calimala Guild. Go down via
Calimala to piazza della Repubblica.

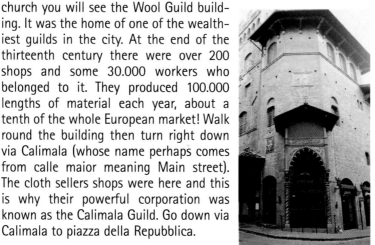

PIAZZA DELLA REPUBBLICA

In Roman times the forum stood here in what was the central area of the city, where all the most important public functions took place.

The two main streets, the cardo and the decumanus intersected here. The point at which they met was the very heart of town and it was marked by a column. When in 1431 it was damaged it was replaced by an important statue representing Plenty, the goddess who protected the merchants.
In 1721, though, the statue fell down and the **column of Abundance** was rebuilt. It still towers over the square today.

In the Middle Ages the most important market in town was held here, the Old market. There were vendors selling all kinds of goods, craftsmen, doctors, notaries and even performing street artists, acrobats and jugglers.
The place was so crowded and so hectic you had to be careful not to be taken in by all the swindlers and charlatans who roamed the area, trying to sell miracle medicines, love potions or other similar tricks.

Go under the big arch and take via degli Strozzi. Soon you will be in front of one of Florence's biggest Palaces.

PALAZZO STROZZI

It is not a medieval palace but its history is nevertheless very interesting. The Strozzi were the arch enemies of the Medici and because of this they were exiled in 1434. However, although they were far from their city they certainly did not give up. Filippo Strozzi, a clever banker, made a fortune for himself in Naples. When they returned to Florence he decided to show the world that he was the richest and most influential man in the city. He bought and demolished all the buildings around his house and finally managed to realise his dream of building the biggest palace in Florence!

It did not bring him much luck though. He died without seeing the job finished.

Now leave the square and take via Monalda on your right. Walk along till you get to via di Porta Rossa.

PALAZZO TORREGIANI

Palazzo Torregiani is at no.19. Until 1559 it belonged to the Bartolini family. It is said that the owner of this house once invited his rival merchants for a drink. He offered them the best wine and laced it with opium, a drug that makes you sleep. The next morning, he was, naturally, the only one to wake up and when a large delivery of goods arrived, and there were no competitors to sell to, he was able to get it all at a good price. This was the beginning of the family's fortune. In fact their motto is "sleep not" and their symbol is the poppy, the flower from which opium is extracted. Can you find their coat of arms?

PALAZZO DAVANZATI

Palazzo Davanzati is at 13 via di Porta Rossa. Now it is the home of the Museo della Casa Fiorentina, the Florentine House Museum.

Connect the iron objects you can see on the wall to their various functions:

1. For flags or torches	2. For hanging out the washing or birdcages	3. For tying up horses

If you go down to a small square you will see on the right the Palazzo dei Capitani of the Guelphs.

In 1268, they formed an organisation to administrate, among other things, the property of the exiled Ghibellines. This became known as the Parte Guelfa. The institution became very powerful and at times carried out terrible reprisals, including that of demolishing the homes of the Ghibellines that stood where the piazza della Signoria is now.

LOGGIA DEL MERCATO NUOVO

Further along you come to the loggia of the Mercato Nuovo, the New Market. It was built in around the middle of the sixteenth century to give the gold and silk merchants and bankers a safe place to carry out their business. It was here that the Municipal officials assayed the gold florin, verifying its authenticity. The marble wheel in the middle of the floor is where dishonest merchants were condemned to the pillory - whoever wished to was free to throw rotten fruit and vegetables at them! The wheel served another purpose too.

It marked the place where the carroccio would be placed. In the Middle Ages, the carroccio was the war coach of the old Municipalities and it was placed there before a battle. Now look for the "porcellino". We'll give you a clue, it's not a pig and it's made of bronze.

1.   Baptistery
2.   Cathedral
3.   Giotto's Bell Tower
4.   Basilica of Santa Maria Novella
5.   Basilica of Santa Croce
6.   Piazzale Michelangelo
7.   San Salvatore al Monte
8.   Basilica of San Miniato

MEDIEVAL FLORENCE
PLACES OF WORSHIP

Baptistery: weekdays 12-18.30, holidays 8.30-13.30

Santa Maria del Fiore: weekdays 10-17, holidays 13-17;
1st Saturday of the month 10-15.30

Cathedral bell tower: 1 April-31 October 9-18.50;
1 November-31 March 9-16.20;

Santa Maria Novella: 7-12.15,15-18;
Saturday 7-12.15, 15-17;

Santa Croce: summer 8-18.30; winter 8-12.30, 15-18.30;

Opera di Santa Croce Museum:
1 April-31 October: 10-12.30, 14.30-18.30;
1 November-31 March: 10-12.30, 15-17

San Miniato al Monte: summer 8-12, 14-19;
winter 8-12, 14.30-18

This walk leads you through the city's religious centres and some of the most important areas of Medieval Florence.

In around the IV century after Christ, the Roman city fell into decline and the few remaining inhabitants went to live near the places of worship. On the site where the Duomo now stands a church was built which then became the cathedral of the city (i.e. the seat of the bishop). It was dedicated to St. Reparata, who was considered the saviour of Florence.

Legend tells that the barbarous Ostrogoths who laid siege to the city were defeated on her saint's day - 8 October, and that Reparata appeared in the sky waving a standard bearing a lily.

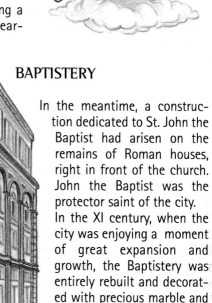

BAPTISTERY

In the meantime, a construction dedicated to St. John the Baptist had arisen on the remains of Roman houses, right in front of the church. John the Baptist was the protector saint of the city.

In the XI century, when the city was enjoying a moment of great expansion and growth, the Baptistery was entirely rebuilt and decorated with precious marble and mosaics. It was a long and costly task which took over 200 years, but it is considered one of the masterpieces of Romanesque architecture (@12).

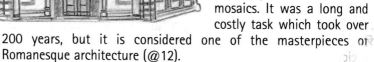

The building was completely covered with slabs of white Carrara marble and green Prato marble placed in such a way as to create

geometric shapes the same on each side. As was often the case with buildings of the time pieces from older buildings were reused. As you walk around the Baptistery look for a rectangular relief with a naval battle

carved on it. It probably belonged to an old sarcophagus.

Now go in to visit the interior. It seems almost as though mosaics and marbles cover every corner of the building. But it is not so! If you look at the floor you will find a bare space. This is where the baptismal font was located. It was demolished in 1576 when Francesco I de' Medici wanted to hold a ceremony to christen his first born son and, to make room for the guests, he replaced the large font with a much smaller one. Can you find it?

The rest of the floor is decorated with marble intarsia, which is a careful interlocking of different marbles to create elegant decorative motifs.

Now look up towards the dome and look for the scene of the Last Judgement. Observe the large figure of Christ the Judge. At his feet men are coming out of their tombs to be judged. They are very very small in order to stress Christ's importance. On the left are those who will go to Heaven and on the right, those going to Hell. In the middle of the dome Christ is surrounded by a host of angels. Beneath these there are scenes like cartoon strips that tell stories from the Bible. Look for God creating the world or Adam and Eve.

All the scenes are on a gold background. The most important thing for the Medieval artists was that the picture should be luminous and ꞏous.

With the passing of time the Baptistery became more and more splendid as its political stature grew. Every year on 24 June (the feast of the baptism of Christ) the wealthy representatives of the Guilds, the feudal lords, governors of the towns under Florentine dominion, all met together. It was the place where knights were named, home of the war coach and that of the trophies of defeated enemies.

By the beginning of the 14th century the old wooden doors were no longer grand enough for such an important building and new bronze ones were deemed necessary. These would cost a great deal more, though. Fortunately the powerful Calimala Guild declared itself willing to pay the bill.

Go outside and look for its coat of arms above one of the doors. This riddle will help you find it.

Among birds it is the strongest, but here you will see it, wings apart, no prey in its mouth but a roll of wool.

The first of the new doors was made in 1336 by Andrea Pisano (1290-1340). It is the one on the via dei Calzaioli side. There are 28 panels each containing a scene from the life of John the Baptist.

When you walk around the building you will come to the San Zanobi column.

The story goes that on 26 January 429 while the dead body of bishop Zanobi was being carried along in a solemn procession to the Cathedral, the pall bearers shook it about so much that the body of the saint touched a dry elm tree along the way and the tree miraculously began to flower again.

The elm became a place of worship from that day on and when it finally died, the column was erected in its place.

Go to the north door, also called the door of the Cross (via Cavour side).

In 1401, in order to decide who should be called to make the new door, the Florentines organ-

Ghiberti

ised a competition. The contestants included Jacopo della Quercia, (1371/4-1438) Filippo Brunelleschi (1377-1446) and Lorenzo Ghiberti (1378-1455). Each of them made a trial panel. In the end it was a tie between Ghiberti and Brunelleschi. Only the first was chosen though, perhaps because Brunelleschi

Brunelleschi

had been more extravagant and had used 7 kilos more bronze. The two trial panels are at the Bargello Museum (@103).

Continue your way round until you get to the door of paradise, so called because Michelangelo stated that it was 'worthy of Paradise.'

In 1425 Florence wanted a third door in bronze. Again Ghiberti was called and given the task. The door was to be placed on the north side, but when it was finished it was so beautiful that it was put on the most impor-tant side, near the Cathedral. It shows scenes from the Old Testament. What you see today is a copy. Some of the original panels are at the Opera del Duomo Museum now.

In comparison with the panels on the pre-vious door these are:
T = TRUE   F = FALSE
1. bigger   T   F
2. different shapes   T   F
3. more crowded   T   F
4. the figures are portrayed in
   less detail   T   F

CATHEDRAL OF SANTA MARIA DEL FIORE

Reconstruction of the Baptistery was a cause of great pride among the people of the city. Now, by comparison, the Cathedral seemed rather clumsy to the Florentines. Santa Reparata, as it was still called, was however still the principal place of worship in the city. It had been restored on various occasions, buildings had sprung up around it to house pilgrims and it was the burial place of the city's most influential inhabitants. All the major religious ceremonies were held there and emperors and popes visited it.

At the end of the 13th century almost the whole city underwent restructuring and improvements and it was decided that a new Cathedral was necessary, one that would equal those in the nearby cities. The Prior government called Arnolfo di Cambio (1245-1302) to design the church, which was to take the name of Santa Maria in Fiore, thereby linking the name of the Madonna to the flower symbol of Florence. Various buildings were demolished to make room for it and the old church was incorporated into the new one.

I thought we'd have a balcony!

On 8 September 1296, the digging of the foundations began, but Arnolfo died at the beginning of the 1300's and work stopped. Only the façade and side walls had been completed. The mark . of the famous Arnolfo was to remain however. It was his idea to place alternating green, red and white marble on the exterior, thereby linking it to the design of the Baptistery but adding a third colour.

After Arnolfo's death, Giotto (ca.1267-1337) was called to direct the works but he dedicated most of his time to the bell tower, so that the works stopped for almost 20 years!

In the meantime Arnolfo's project was modified. The interior of the church was to be changed and the dome widened. It was to measure 41 metres in diameter and 55 metres in height – it would be the biggest in the world. It seemed almost impossible though to cover such a vast space with a single structure and, indeed, for a good 25 years the cathedral had no dome. There was no artist able to achieve such a feat! One of the ideas was to build up a sort of hill made of earth and coins onto which the dome would be "thrown"; the people called to recover the coins would take the earth away with them too!

In 1418 a competition was held to try to solve the problem. Ghiberti and Brunelleschi who had already met before during the one for the Baptistery doors, found themselves pitted against one another again, and again the outcome was a tie. Ghiberti soon gave up the idea of the task, leaving Brunelleschi alone with the greatest challenge of his life.

In secret, he planned a dome that could be built in a void, so that scaffolding 55 metres high became unnecessary. Want to know how he did it?

The internal structure or framework which essentially supports the entire dome is composed of 8 large vertical ribs that start from the top of the octagon. Then there are 16 secondary ribs. The ribs are connected by rings of horizontal strips made of brick.

The dome is made up of 2 spherical vaults, one

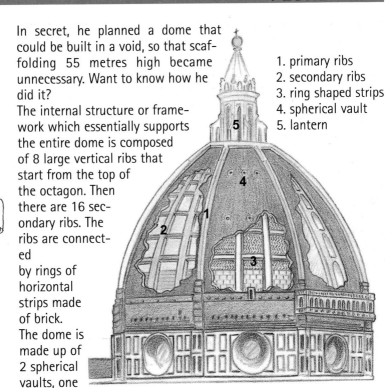

1. primary ribs
2. secondary ribs
3. ring shaped strips
4. spherical vault
5. lantern

external and one internal, built up with materials that get lighter as they go higher: stone at the bottom, brick further up.

The workers raised the dome by continuously adding concentric rings of brick. The bricks were slotted into one another using the 'herringbone' technique, so that each row was self-supporting. It was the first time anyone had thought to do this. Brunelleschi invented new systems and new machinery that would move and raise the materials with greater ease.

Finally, the lantern, a small temple-shaped structure, was placed on top of the dome. It brings the total height to 106 metres and is not purely decorative at all. It prevents the pressure of the ribs from causing the dome to collapse! In 1436 the dome was finally terminated and on 25 March a church was consecrated that was "raised above the skies, wide enough to cover all the people of Tuscany with its shade", "erta sopra e'ceili, ampla da coprire chon sua ombra tutti e popoli toscani".

Still today it is one of the 5 highest domes in the world, together with St. Peter's and the Pantheon in Rome, St. Paul's in London and Santa Sofia in Istanbul.

Go into the cathedral. As you can see it is in the shape of a large cross. Here we can see many elements of Gothic architecture (@12). Nowadays the church is almost bare but you should try to imagine it full of works of art and crowds of people.

Not only was it the most important church in Florence but it was also a place where people would meet to exchange ideas, or hold political ceremonies.

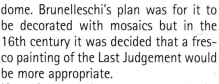

Go first towards the right aisle to the steps (1) between the first and second pilasters. Here you can go down and take a look at what remains of the old Santa Reparata church. Just think, the people of Florence were so attached to her that they continued calling the cathedral by her name until it was made compulsory in 1412 to call it Santa Maria in Fiore.

Go back upstairs and walk along the nave until you are beneath the dome. Brunelleschi's plan was for it to be decorated with mosaics but in the 16th century it was decided that a fresco painting of the Last Judgement would be more appropriate.

If you feel up to it, you can go up to the dome (2), a little tiring perhaps but fun. On the walls of the church are portraits of famous Florentines.

Look along the left aisle (3) for a painting on wood that celebrates Florence's greatest literary man, Dante Alighieri (@ 36).

Further on, you will come across the painted equestrian statues of two famous 14th century condottieri (4) Giovanni Acuto, painted by Paolo Uccello (1436) and Niccolò da Tolentino by Andrea del Castagno (1456).

Before you leave you can see what Brunelleschi looked like (5).

GIOTTO'S BELL TOWER

It is named after Giotto because it was initially designed by him, but in actual fact it was built by three great artists of the 14th century, Giotto, Andrea Pisano and Francesco Talenti.

It was started in 1334 but at the time of Giotto's death in 1337 not even the first floor had been completed. Andrea Pisano built the second floor, but he made a variation. What was it?

> 1. he used different coloured marbles
> 2. he added mosaics
> 3. he added niches for statues

In 1350 Talenti became director of works and, with the addition of the last three floors, he completed the task. In the upper part he put in large windows; notice how as they move upwards the openings lengthen. The top openings are different from the others.

How?	1. they have not got a pediment	2. they are divided into three parts	3. they are not pointed

There are 2 other buildings in the square whose histories are very old.

CONFRATERNITY OF THE MISERICORDIA

The seat of the confraternity of the Misericordia is to the side of the bell tower. It started at the end of the 13th century to transport the wounded or ill, and it still performs this function today. The building has been renewed, so now it has a modern look.

COMPAGNIA DEL BIGALLO

At the beginning of via Calzaioli is the seat of the Compagnia del Bigallo.

It was built during the middle of the 14th century and, in its first years, abandoned babies were put on view beneath its arcades.

PIAZZA SANTA MARIA NOVELLA

Go towards via dei Pecori, then go down via degli Agli and via del Trebbio. At the end of this street you will come across a column with a cross on top of it. Take via delle Belle Donne, the road in front of you and go along until you get to Santa Maria Novella.

The religious orders were fundamental to the development of Medieval Florence. At the time, the people listened with ever increasing enthusiasm to the new ways of living as Christians being taught by the brotherhood.

These new orders differed from the previous ones because rather than leading their spiritual lives in isolated abbeys far from the city and its people, these settled in the town centres and made a point of being in constant contact with the inhabitants. They chose to establish themselves in sites around which there were wide spaces where they could preach to the crowds, reunite large numbers of people and perform acts of charity. It was near these large squares that the popular quarters grew up.

At the end of the century the confraternity churches were equal to the city's major public buildings in both size and political stature. In Florence the most important are Santa Maria Novella, which is run by the Dominican fathers and Santa Croce, run by the Franciscans.

Novella is by far the best!

No, no, Santa Croce is!

BASILICA OF SANTA MARIA NOVELLA

In 1221 a Dominican friar, Giovanni da Salerno, arrived in the city with several of his fellow brothers. They established themselves in a small church called Santa Maria delle Vigne, which stood outside the city walls in an area surrounded by rows of vines. Although it was outside Florence, the area was not uninhabited.

The poorest people, along with those who had recently arrived, lived around the walls. They were usually workers in the service of the powerful merchants of the major Guilds.

The site chosen by the Dominicans had a large open space in front of it which was modernised to accomodate the crowds that hastened to listen to the preachers.

Building of the new church, called Santa Maria Novella, is said to have begun in 1278. Two Dominican fathers, Sisto and Ristoro are thought to have been responsible for the project. Initially, work proceeded quickly, but then it stopped and the façade was left incomplete. Finally, in 1458 a very wealthy nobleman, Giovanni Paolo Rucellai agreed to pay for the work to be completed and entrusted the job to the great architect Leon Batista Alberti (1406-1472). He was faced with a difficult task: to complete the façade without creating too strong a contrast with the parts already completed, using a different style.

He came up with the idea of the two large volutes that you see in the upper part. These recall some of the older elements (geometric divisions and the colours of the marble) and at the same time conceal the most contrasting ones (the pointed Gothic features), creating a new yet very harmonious ensemble.

Giovanni Rucellai, so as to make known to everyone that he had been the one to finance the completion of the church, not only had his family coat of arms placed on the façade, but also had his own personal emblem of a full sail included. Can you find them?

Go into the church. The interior is one of the most famous examples of Florentine Gothic (@12).

Santa Maria Novella is a monastery church, but it is large and full of light. It was not created only for silent meditation but also as a meeting place for large congregations. Originally it did have a part reserved for the monks and the walls were decorated with frescoes that acted as real 'illustrated stories', to be understood also by those who were unable to read.

Behind you to the right of the door is one of the few remaining original frescoes (1): it represents the archangel Gabriel announcing the birth of Jesus to Mary.

Try putting the scenes in the panels below in the right order and find the odd one out:

1. Adoration of the Magi
2. Birth of Jesus
3. Baptism of Jesus
4. Multiplication of the loaves and fishes

Have you noticed how many details the artist painted in the main scene to show us that it takes place in Mary's house?

Which of these are not in the fresco?

Now go along the left aisle. As you walk along, notice how many coats of arms there are set in the floor. They are tombs, some of which are extremely old.

Go to the **Strozzi chapel (2)**. It was paid for by a very rich man and usurer called Tommaso di Rosello Strozzi who hoped in this way to receive pardon for his sinful practices. It was decorated by Nardo di Cione (mid 14th century). At the centre is the Last Judgement, on the left Paradise and on the right, Hell. Notice how dramatically life after death is portrayed. This can be partly attributed to the fact that the work was executed shortly after the end of a terrible plague that decimated the population of Florence in 1348.

Among the hundreds of angel and saint figures in the fresco representing paradise, near the centre on the left there is a personage whose poetry tells of a journey through the world of the dead. Which of the three is he?

Dante   Virgil   Homer

In front of the altar is a large polyptych (from the Greek polys = many and ptychòs = fold, a painting on several boards connected together) painted by Andrea di Cione, called Orcagna. In the centre is Christ enthroned with around him angels, Mary and several of the major saints.

Try to see which ones you can recognise and link them to the symbol that portrays their mission or martyrdom.

1. St. Peter   2. St. Thomas   3. St. George   4. St. Catherine   5. St. Paul
A. wheel   B. sword and dragon   C. keys   D. Holy books   E. sword and books

Now if you go back along the nave you will come to a fresco **(3)** painted by a great artist named Masaccio in around 1427. It represents the **Trinity**: in the centre is Christ on the Cross, at the bottom are the Madonna and St. John, at the top God the Father and beneath his beard is the Holy Spirit in the form of a dove.

It seems almost as if the painting embraces the spectator, making them feel 'inside' the scene. To create this effect Masaccio used a way of representing objects in space called perspective. It will characterise most of the works of the Renaissance (@12).

If you look carefully at the painting you will notice that someone has entered the scene. It is the Lenzi family (who commissioned it). They did not only wish to be portrayed near the holy figures, but also to be painted the same size, something that would have been unthinkable until shortly before!

Masaccio lived and worked during the Renaissance, a period in which man found greater faith in himself and his own capabilities. He was also better able to face both earthly life and the hereafter without the great fear of the Medieval man.

Whatever have you done?

Another great artist of the Renaissance was Brunelleschi, brilliant architect and clever sculptor.

Towards the end of the church **(4)** is a refined wooden Crucifix, carved by him in 1420. He is said to have sculpted it in answer to the one executed by Donatello for the Santa Croce church. He did not approve of Donatello's Christ because he found it too realistic and is said to have protested "You've crucified a peasant!"

Over the centuries the interior of the church was changed on a number of occasions. When this happened, the works of art were moved about (Giotto's Crucifix ended up in the sacristy), while others were even destroyed.

Here we go again - move it here, take it there...

At the end of the 15th century Domenico Ghirlandaio (1449-1494) was commissioned to decorate the **apse (5)**. On the left wall he painted scenes from the life of Mary, and on the right one stories from the life of John the Baptist, patron saint of Florence.

Among Ghirlandaio's helpers was a young artist called Michelangelo who some say painted these small figures. Look for them among the

many people that crowd the apse. During the times when these frescoes were carried out, the power of the most influential members of society was affirmed by exhibition of their wealth. This is why the artists who were in the service of the great families were careful to include the most minute details of their luxurious clothes, jewels, head dresses and fine buildings. The person who financed the work of art would always appear in one of the scenes, so that everyone knew who had put up the money. These particular frescoes were paid for by an extremely wealthy man named Giovanni Tornabuoni who, not content merely to appear in the holy scenes alone, was accompanied by friends and relatives. In the scene of **Mary's visit to Elizabeth** you can see Diadora Tornabuoni, Giovanni's sister, on the right.

She is wearing a blue dress and a white veil and she has a delicate little nose. In the birth of John the Baptist another sister appears, Lucrezia Tornabuoni (you will recognise her by her nose too).

Which of the three is Lucrezia's son?

Michelangelo   *Lorenzo de' Medici*   *Dante*

PIAZZA SANTA CROCE

During the Middle Ages this area was marshy and unhealthy since it was flooded frequently by the river Arno. Only the very poor lived there. At the beginning of the XIII century Franciscan fathers settled here in a small chapel with a wide open space before it where they could preach.

Subsequently, a monastery and a school were established, where the sons of the most important families went to study.

However, before long it was decided to erect a larger church dedicated to the Santa Croce, the Holy Cross . It became one of the major religious centres in the city, so important in fact that soon building began on the great basilica you see today.

Santa Croce was consecrated in 1443, still incomplete, after many years of often interrupted work. The façade belongs to the 19th century. The Florentines did not meet in the square only for religious services. Indeed, until the 14th century games, tournaments and popular festivals were held there. It was even used as a football pitch. There are circular pieces of marble on the façades of two of the buildings on the long sides of the square -these marked mid- field!

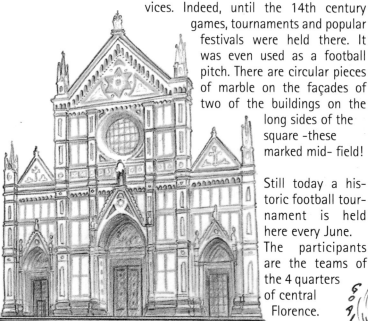

Still today a historic football tournament is held here every June. The participants are the teams of the 4 quarters of central Florence.

BASILICA OF SANTA CROCE

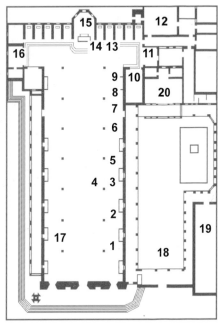

When you go in it seems immense. So as to create a building big enough to accommodate large crowds Arnolfo di Cambio made it so wide that it was impossible to use stone vaults to cover the entire ceiling so for the nave he used wooden beams, which formed a hut-shaped structure. Like the cathedral and Santa Maria Novella, this church is in the Gothic style (@12).

Santa Croce is much loved by the people of Florence and is famous all over the world not only because of the works of art that are housed in it, but also because all the most illustrious men of the city are either buried or remembered here. Wealthy citizens paid large sums of money to be buried here, others are great artists, literary men, musicians or scientists.

Along the right aisle , beyond the first altar is: the tomb (1) of Michelangelo Buonarroti (1475-1564), the artist to whom his contemporaries had already attributed the word "divine". When Michelangelo died in Rome, pope Clement VII wanted him to be buried in St. Peter's, but the artist's nephew quickly had his body taken to Florence, where the whole city rushed to pay homage to him.

Who are the three women weeping on his tomb?
1. the three Graces
2. his three sisters
3. painting, sculpture and architecture

Continuing you will come to **Dante's cenotaph (2)**, a funeral monument that does not contain the body of the dead person. Dante died in exile in Ravenna and was buried there (@36).

The Florentines tried in every way to get back the body of the greatest poet of all times. In the 16th century Michelangelo promised that if Dante were returned to Florence he would sculpt a magnificent tomb for him.

However when the people of Ravenna were finally convinced to open his tomb it was empty! All that was left were a few bones and some laurel leaves. In 1865, it was decided to knock down a wall to enlarge his burial place. Behind the wall

Alfieri

they found a casket with "Dante's bones" written on it. Inside the casket was a parchment scroll with an explanation by two monks who, afraid that 'their' Dante might be taken back to the city that had so cruelly exiled him, wrote that they had removed his remains and put them in a safe place.

Further on you can see the **(3) tomb of poet Vittorio Alfieri** (1749-1803) made by Antonio Canova (1757-1822), an artist that always looked for harmony, composure and the ideal beauty of the classical art world. Opposite, on the pilaster, is one of Santa Croce's most famous pieces of art, a **pulpit (4)** by Benedetto da Maiano (1442-1497), showing scenes from the life of St.Francis. Next you come to the **tomb (5) of Niccolò Machiavelli** (1469-1527), an important philosopher who thought a great deal about the best ways to govern.

Machiavelli

After a relief of the **Annunciation (6)** by Donatello is the **tomb of Leonardo Bruni (7)**, a powerful personage of 15th century Florence. It is the work of Bernardo Rossellino (1409-1464) and it was so popular that it served as a model for numerous future artists: "the deceased man is represented lying on his bed, dressed as a man of letters of antiquity within a space reminiscent of classical architecture".

Which elements do not come from the classical world?
1. lions
2. cherubs
3. capitals
4. cat
5. winged women

Rossini

The next **tombs (8 and 9) are those of Gioachino Rossini** (1792-1868), one of Italy's greatest composers, and **Ugo Foscolo** (1778-1827), a key poet and man of letters of the 19th century.

Now you have reached the transept (the arms of the cross in a cross-shaped church); on the right is the **Castellani or Santissimo chapel (10)**. It was frescoed at the end of the 14th century by Agnolo Gaddi and shows the lives of the major saints.

Foscolo

In the 18th century, when Medieval painting was considered 'barbaric', the walls of this chapel and those of the ones near the main altar were whitewashed, causing almost irreparable damage to their valuable frescoes.

Go on to the **Baroncelli chapel (11)**. It was decorated by Taddeo Gaddi, Giotto's most promising pupil, with scenes from the life of the Virgin Mary. Look for the scene where the angel appears to the sleeping shepherds. It may be the first ever night scene to be painted in a fresco. In the same chapel you will also see the polyptych with the Incoronation of the Virgin. It is signed by Giotto, although a number of different artists worked on it.

Go into the **sacristy (12)**. Here you will see the Passion, Crucifixion and Death of Christ. Notice how simple and clear the way of portraying these scenes is. The works that decorated the churches of the mendicant orders needed to be easy to understand because most people could not read. They were like sermons in picture form.

Where is this personage hidden?

Look for this golden frame. It is said to contain the habit of St.Francis.

Go out of the sacristy and proceed to the **Peruzzi chapel (13)**. It was decorated by Giotto (1267 ca.-1337) between 1320 and 1328. It shows the life of St. John the Baptist and St. John the Evangelist. The frescoes are in very poor condition because of the 18th century whitewashing.

WHAT!

TUNICA

In the **Bardi chapel (14)** Giotto painted the life of St. Francis. Look on the left how he showed the death of the saint: the faces and bodies of the monks express the deep pain they are feeling.

Go to the **Maggiore chapel (15)**, which is different in size from all the others. The upward surge seems to lead the eyes of the faithful towards the heart of the church.

Now go to the second **Bardi di Verno chapel (16)**. Donatello's famous wooden Crucifix hangs over the altar (@59).

Retrace your steps along the nave. You will see more funeral monuments, the last of which is **(17) the tomb of Galileo Galilei (1564-1642)**, the scientist that studied the stars. He said that it was the earth that went round the sun and not the other way round. Because of his beliefs he was put in prison by the Church and it was only a few years ago that it admitted its mistakes and reinstated him.

Galileo Galilei

Now leave the church and go into the **cloisters (18)**. Go to where the

refectory of the monastery was. This was the room where the monks ate and which today is the **Opera di Santa Croce museum (19)** During the disastrous flood of 1966, the water reached a height of 6 metres, causing terrible damage to the building and works of art.

Go in and look for the famous **Crucifix** painted by Giotto's master Cimabue (1240-1302). When pope Paul VI came to visit Florence after the flood, he kneeled before the damaged Crucifix and paid homage to what had become the symbol of the city's 'wounds'.

Leave the refectory and go in the direction of the **Pazzi chapel (20)**,

an architectural masterpiece of the 15th century. It was started by Brunelleschi in around 1430 for Andrea de'Pazzi.
The Pazzi family are remembered for a bloody conspiracy they were involved in.

In 1469, after the death of Cosimo, who had been the

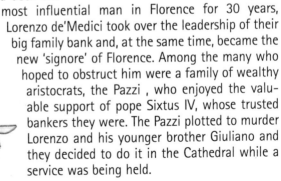

most influential man in Florence for 30 years, Lorenzo de'Medici took over the leadership of their big family bank and, at the same time, became the new 'signore' of Florence. Among the many who hoped to obstruct him were a family of wealthy aristocrats, the Pazzi , who enjoyed the valuable support of pope Sixtus IV, whose trusted bankers they were. The Pazzi plotted to murder Lorenzo and his younger brother Giuliano and they decided to do it in the Cathedral while a service was being held.

It was 26 April 1478. The conspirators waited for an agreed sign, then assaulted Giuliano, murdering him with 19 stab wounds. In the

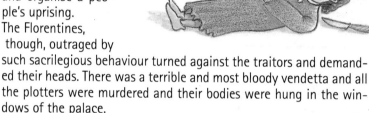

meanwhile, Lorenzo, who was attacked by two monks in on the plot, was protected by his most faithful followers, ready to lay down their lives for him.

Lorenzo fled to the sacristy and hid as the other conspirators tried in vain to take palazzo Vecchio and organise a people's uprising.

The Florentines, though, outraged by such sacrilegious behaviour turned against the traitors and demanded their heads. There was a terrible and most bloody vendetta and all the plotters were murdered and their bodies were hung in the windows of the palace.

From that moment on, no one dared to question Lorenzo's steadily rising political power; a power that caused him to be known as Lorenzo the Magnificent.

Go into the chapel. The building's harmonious proportions are emphasised by the white of the walls and grey of the clear stone. The

only touches of colour are the glazed terracotta medallions. Note the Apostles along the walls and the 4 Evangelists up above. These masterpieces are examples of an unusual technique that Florentine sculptor Luca della Robbia (1400-1482) and his nephew Andrea (1435-1525) used for decoration. The brilliant colours and their durability made this method of working clay a world famous art.

PIAZZALE MICHELANGELO

This wide open space is dedicated to Michelangelo Buonarroti who, during the 1530 siege of Florence encircled the hill with walls in order to defend the city below more effectively. From here there is a magnificent view. On your right is the hill of Fiesole and , down in the valley, Florence.

Which of these buildings is not part of the view in front of you ?

Now, with your back to the city, go up the long flight of steps to the right of the loggia.

SAN SALVATORE AL MONTE

The church you come to is the 16th century San Salvatore al Monte. It was designed by Florentine architect Simone del Pollaiolo (1457-1508). It is a simple building with little decoration. Partly because of this and also because it was then in open countryside, Michelangelo called it "the beautiful little villa". Now, if you go to the right of the church, you will come to three roads. If you take the one on the left you will come to the fortifications that protected the hill. In 1530, in the hurry to defend the city from Charles V's imperial troops, Michelangelo had had the walls erected quickly in flattened earth and rough brick. Later they were rebuilt and made more resistant. Above the entrance arch is a coat of arms you will often see as you wander around Florence. It is the emblem of the Medici family.

BASILICA OF SAN MINIATO AL MONTE

Go into the fortress and continue until you get to the square in front of San Miniato.

You are looking at one of Florence's oldest churches. According to tradition, it was built near the tomb of Miniato, an Armenian prince who had travelled to Florence to spread Christianity and who was martyred in 250 A.D. during the reign of emperor Decius. The legend goes that after the saint was decapitated on the banks of the Arno river, he picked up his head, put it under his arm and went up the hill, because he wanted to be buried on the site where he had lived as a hermit. From then on, it became a place of pilgrimage and worship, and by the IX century a church and a monastery had already been built there.

When you go in, you will see the date "1207" written on the ground. This was when the building work was completed - it took nearly 200 years!

Right from the time of its construction, the church had close links with the city. During the siege of 1530, the bell tower was used as a watch tower and Michelangelo padded it with bales of hay and mattresses to protect it from cannon fire. In 1600 it was used as a hospital and, later as a hospice for the poor. In 1875 the fortified area around the church was turned into a cemetery. Carlo Collodi, the creator of Pinocchio, is buried here. Look at the façade. It is considered a masterpiece of Romanesque architecture (@12). It is very orderly and is divided into many different parts by means of a decoration known as intarsia. In the upper part is a mosaic on a gold background in which Christ, accompanied by the Virgin Mary and St. Miniato, raises his hand in a gesture of blessing and welcoming to those entering the church.

Go into the church now, walk along the nave and have a look at what remains of the famous marble 13th century floor. Here too, the intarsia method has been used. Walking along the nave, look for the fig-

ures of the zodiac on the ground. The word zodiac comes from the Greek and means 'containing figures of animals'. The zodiac signs are in fact names that we have given to groups of stars that, seen from the earth, seem to form shapes that are almost always animal-like.

When you look around you at the interior of this church, you will notice that it is on three levels - the nave level, the raised area where the altar is and, finally, that of the crypt, below the altar. This means that the central altar is exactly above St. Miniato's tomb, the most important place in the church.

At the end of the nave is the **chapel of the Crucifix,** planned in the mid 15th century to house the miraculous crucifix of St. John Gualberto.

The tale goes that John was undecided whether or not to forgive his brother's murderer. When he eventually decided to be merciful, he turned to face the crucifix and Christ lowered his head in sign of approval. John was so profoundly moved by this miracle that he pardoned the murderer and became a monk in the San Miniato monastery.

Now you can go down into the **crypt,** which is the oldest and most fascinating part of the basilica. Look up at the ceiling.
It has not got a wooden ceiling like the rest of the church, but a brick vault. Not only was this considered more beautiful, it was also a lot more fireproof.

The vaulting is supported by small columns, each one different from the other. From the end of the Roman period onwards - IV century A.D. - it was customary to use mate-

rials from earlier buildings for both decoration and construction, but it was not always possible to find enough columns of the same type. However, it was cheaper this way, the materials were ready to use and the buildings were made more prestigious.

Now go up to see the apse windows. You will notice that they are all covered with thin layers of alabaster. These were to soften the light inside the church so that the monks could pray with greater concentration. You will also have noticed that the pulpit is set sideways and is located above the wall that divides the church into two.

Repent you evil lot!

OH

This was so that it could be seen by both the monks and the congregation who was this side of the wall and was not allowed into the apse area, where the altar was.

The pulpit is the small balcony from which the sermon was held. In fact in Italian there is an expression that says "just look from which pulpit the sermon is coming".

This expression means:
1. someone who preaches well but rummages about at the same time
2. someone who judges others but behaves badly himself
3. a priest who preaches from the pulpit

Now try imagining being in the Middle Ages. You are attending a service, the light is suffused, you cannot see either the monks or the priest, only the big mosaic at the end of the apse lit up by thousands of candles and, in the background, hear the singing of the monks. It must have been an exceptionally evocative atmosphere and you still get a feel of it today when the church choir sings. If you would like to hear it ask in the sacristy for information.

LAUDATE

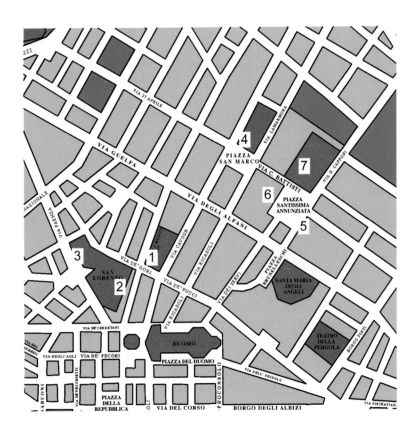

1.   Palazzo Medici Riccardi
2.   San Lorenzo Basilica
3.   Medici Chapels
4.   San Marco Monastery
5.   Ospedale degli Innocenti
6.   Serviti Loggia
7.   Santissima Annunciata Church

RENAISSANCE FLORENCE: THE MEDICI QUARTER

Medici or Magi Chapels:	9-13, 15-18; holidays 9-13 (closed Wednesdays)
San Lorenzo Basilica:	7-12, 15.30-18.30
Laurenziana Library:	9-13
Medici Chapel: New Sacristy, Chapel of the Princes	8.30-17; Sunday 8.30-13.50 (closed 1st, 3rd, 5th Monday and 2nd and 4th Sunday of the month)
San Marco Museum:	8.30-13.50 (closed 2nd and 4th Monday and 1st and 3rd Sunday of the month)

FLORENCE IN THE RENAISSANCE

At the end of the 14th century, in order to put an end to the continuous fighting between the various families and overcome the serious economic crisis that had hit the city, the Florentines created an oligarchy (from the Greek oligos few, that is formed of a limited number of people), led by the Albizi family.

But the peace did not last long. Soon the Albizzi family were in conflict with another powerful family, the Medici. Giovanni di Bicci de' Medici was at that time the wealthiest man in the city. His bank lent money even to the pope and the emperor. It seemed clear that his son Cosimo would become part of the government. However, the Albizi, fearing his power and wealth, had him exiled to Venice, where he was received with great honour nonetheless.

Many people in Florence were sorry to lose his money and prestige, so that only a year later, the Albizi themselves were forced to leave. Cosimo returned to the city and regained power.

Although Cosimo, later known as the Elder, his son Piero and nephew Lorenzo all governed Florence with no official roles, they were effectively its undisputed rulers.

In the 15th century Florence continued to gener-

ate new works of art but, while in the Middle Ages the most important ones were financed by the Municipality or the Guilds, now it was the single families that paid for them.

Donatello

Alberti

The most influential families realised that the best way of showing off their wealth and power was to link their name to works of art that everyone could admire and use. Consequently, they build churches and monasteries, paid and patronised writers, poets, artists and architects. They built new palaces and buildings that added to the beauty of the city, studied Greek and Latin and collected vast quantities of old and modern works of art. This period was known as the Renaissance, because it marked the end of the Middle Ages and the rebirth of art and culture (@ 12).

Brunelleschi

Ghiberti

Unlike Romanesque and Gothic, the style of this period did not come from outside, but was born right here in Florence. At the time it was one of the most important art centres in Europe and it was here that the greatest artists of the time lived, namely Brunelleschi, Masaccio, Alberti, Donatello, Ghiberti, Leonardo, Michelangelo and Raphael.

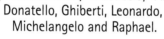

Leonardo

Yet despite this age of splendour, the conspiracies continued to flourish as well.

In 1494 Lorenzo the Magnificent's son Piero gave several castles to the king of France.

Michelangelo

Raffaello

The people, indignant at Piero's weakness, exiled him from Florence, besieged and looted palazzo Medici. Once again Florence became a free republic.

Initially it was led by the Dominican friar Girolamo Savonarola who in previous years had earned the respect of the people by bravely speaking out against the Medici's extravagance.

Soon though, his intransigence began to annoy the great families and the merchants began to worry, among other things, about the pope's opposition. On 8 April 1498, Savonarola was arrested and shortly after was put to death in piazza Signoria. For a while the people's government continued to rule the city even without the leadership of the monk.

It was in this period that Michelangelo sculpted the David, symbol of the Republic that had succeeded in defeating its most powerful enemies. Indeed Florence's enemies were plentiful and extremely dangerous. The Medici could, for instance, rely on the help of the Holy Roman emperor Charles V.

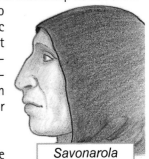

Savonarola

After a period of uncertainty, in 1530 the Medici took back the reins of the government, this time officially. The emperor gave Cosimo I de'Medici the title of Grand duke. Tuscany became a grand duchy and the Medici its lords and rulers. Thanks to his powerful alliances Cosimo was able to increase the territories of the grand duchy, subjecting even its rival Siena. The family moved to palazzo della Signoria and soon after to the magnificent residence built especially for them, the Pitti Palace. During this period new works of art were commissioned and grandiose palaces and princely villas were built.

The Medici governed until the mid 18th century, always allied with the major European states.

Some of the Medici villas

Behind all this splendour however, there was a serious economic crisis. New taxes were introduced to pay for all the luxury and expenses of the court, and these were particularly crippling for the poor.

In 1737 Giangastone died without heirs, leaving Tuscany with a new and grave economic crisis on its hands and effectively with no government. The European rulers then decided that the grand duchy would be handed over to the Austrian Hapsburg-Lorraine family.

Francis-Stephen of Lorraine (1737-1765) and above all his son Peter Leopold (1765-1792) brought about many changes: they reduced court expenditure, removed certain taxes, abolished the death penalty, set up public schools and gave a boost to commerce.

In 1799 Napoleon Bonaparte's troops occupied Florence, expelling the Lorraine. But after the defeat and exile of the French emperor in 1814, the family returned to govern the city, not without having to face numerous attempts at revolt by the people, though. Finally, in 1859 the Lorraine abandoned Florence. Following a vote in which all the population took part, the Tuscans decided to become part of the kingdom of Piedmont-Sardinia. Between 1865 and 1871 Florence was capital of the kingdom of Italy. The city was extended and altered; the old walls were knocked down, hundreds of homes, lanes, towers and small churches disappeared, making space for wide avenues and more functional buildings. During the Second World War, Florence suffered great damage. In August 1944 the withdrawing Nazi troops mined all the old bridges, except for the ponte Vecchio.

On 4 November 1966 the city was flooded by the waters of the overflowing Arno. It caused immense damage to houses and works of art. Thousands of volunteers came from all over Italy to save a heritage that is now considered to belong to the whole of humanity.

THE MEDICI QUARTER

From the 15th century onwards the new political situation affected the way the city was built. The powerful families divided the city into influential areas, where they modernised religious buildings and constructed imposing buildings to show off their importance.

PALAZZO MEDICI RICCARDI

In the 14th century the Medici lived in the area of the Old market. As their power grew though they began to plan a more prestigious residence. Cosimo the Elder chose the area to the north of the Cathedral where he had several properties. In a certain sense he 'restructured' the entire area along a road known as Larga, because of its size. Nowadays this is via Cavour.

Cosimo called Filippo Brunelleschi to design his new palace. Brunelleschi, who was the greatest architect working at that time in Florence, designed a grandiose palace but Cosimo rejected it. He wished to assert his power more discreetly: a palace that was grander than those of the other families would have been too obvious and would have aroused a great deal of envy. So he turned to Michelozzo Michelozzi who had remained loyal to him and had followed him during his exile.

Oh Cosimo ... the project!

Palazzo Medici is at the beginning of via Cavour.

It is easily recognisable since it has three floors with rustication that stands out less and less as the height increases. On the corner there is a large stone shield bearing the Medici coat of arms. It is not sure why the family chose red balls as its emblem, but they probably represent medicine tablets because the founder of the family was a doctor (medico in Italian).

After a series of different events, the Medici sold the palace in 1659 to the marquis Riccardi for the sum of 20.000 scudi. He made numerous changes and doubled its size. Today it is the seat of the Prefecture. Go into the courtyard. The building is constructed in the Renaissance style (@12). Being such a large

building, there was a risk of it becoming rather overwhelming, so it was made as inviting as possible by breaking up the space into regular and harmonious parts.

MAGI OR MEDICI CHAPEL

If you cross the courtyard you will come to a garden with sculptures and large lemon trees. Here you can buy your ticket for the visit to the Magi Chapel, built inside the palace for private religious services. To get to it, go back to the first courtyard and go up the second staircase on the left. The chapel is very small and the visit only lasts 15 minutes.

The famous frescoes on the walls were painted in 1460 by Benozzo Gozzoli (1420-1497) and were commissioned by Piero il Gottoso, Lorenzo the Magnificent's father.

The frescoes show the journey of the Magi on their way to pay homage to baby Jesus. Gozzoli has interpreted it as an elegant procession with knights, pages, pedigree dogs and hunting leopards. As was usual in the Renaissance, the holy scene is filled with references to contemporary life and to the importance of those who had commissioned the work.

Go into the chapel and meet some of the personages of the time. Look for the following people in the left foreground on the wall opposite the entrance:

1. Sigismondo Pandolfo Malatesta signore of Rimini
2. Galeazzo Sforza, young signore of Milan
3. the now elderly Cosimo (he was 60 at the time)
4. his son Piero il Gottoso on a white horse
5. Benozzo Gozzoli, with the signature Opus Benotii (work by Benozzo) on the red hat in the third row.
6. idealised portrait of Lorenzo the Magnificent.

On the short wall look for the middle-aged king, it is emperor of Constantinople Giovanni VII Paleologo.

On the entrance wall instead, you will see the old king with the face of the patriarch of Constantinople, head of the major church of the East.

BASILICA OF SAN LORENZO

Leave the palace, turn right, then right again and walk to piazza San Lorenzo. You are in front of San Lorenzo, the "family church" of the Medici, which, as you can see, is unfinished.

You try completing the façade

According to tradition, it was built in IV century A.D. thanks to a donation by a wealthy lady named Giuliana. It is thought to have been made a cathedral by St. Ambrose in 393. In the XI century it was restructured and consecrated a second time by pope Niccolò II. At the beginning of the 15th century the wealthiest and most influential business men in the area, led by the Medici, decided to pay for reconstruction work of the church and commissioned Filippo Brunelleschi to carry out the work. Giovanni di Bicci de'Medici, father of Cosimo the Elder, agreed to build a sacristy connected to the church and, after a period of interruption, Cosimo, now responsible for the family's affairs following the death of his father, agreed to finance the restructuring of the whole building, after which it became the official Medici church. Work went ahead slowly and the façade was in fact never terminated despite numerous projects by great artists. Here you see Michelangelo's design of 1520.

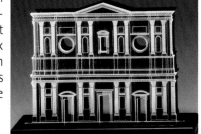

Go into the basilica. It has a cross-shaped plan and is divided into three aisles by columns with Corinthian capitals that remind us of those in classical temples. Brunelleschi added certain elements that later became typical to Renaissance architecture (@ 12): rounded arches, a coffered central ceiling and serena stone (a grey stone from the Fiesole quarries).

Beneath the last two arches of the nave you can see the "pergami" by Donatello (1386-1466); these were pulpits which the priest used for his sermons. The bronze panels contain scenes of the passion of Christ and the martyrdom of St. Lawrence.

Look for three grates with coats of arms and the inscription pater patriae (father of the nation) in front of the main altar: these mark the spot where Cosimo the Elder is buried in the crypt below.

OLD SACRISTY

A large door with intarsia at the end of the church on the left leads to the Old sacristy. This too is by Brunelleschi who here has introduced a new kind of architecture. It is a small cubic room with a perfect half-spherical dome. This is called an umbrella dome and is divided into segments just like an umbrella.

The decorative work is by Donatello.

The parents of Cosimo the Elder, Giovanni de' Bicci and Piccarda Bueri are buried here (under the table in the centre of the room), and Cosimo's two sons (in the tomb to the left of the entrance).

There we are!

LAURENZIANA LIBRARY

When you leave the sacristy go back to the first cloister. You can get to the Laurenziana library from here.

Cosimo the Elder, a great banker and able politician, also loved collecting precious objects. So during the period of his exile he spent a lot of his time collecting books and rare manuscripts. He bought so many that he had to set up several libraries. His successors shared his passion and the 'family' library contains thousands of priceless works. It was designed by Michelangelo in 1524. It was not the only work done by him for San Lorenzo though.

Perhaps I need a library here.

NEW SACRISTY

Go back and go out. Turn left and go round the church to the entrance of the Medici chapels. As soon as you go in you will find yourself in a low-ceilinged room, go up the stairs at the end on the right, walk through the big room you see and go towards the New sacristy, so called because it is perfectly symmetrical to the Old sacristy. In 1519 pope Leo X (Giovanni de' Medici) and cardinal Giulio de' Medici (later pope Clement VII) commissioned Michelangelo to design a funeral chapel for the tombs of their parents Lorenzo and Giuliano and their two heirs, Giuliano de Nemours and Lorenzo d'Urbino, who died when they were still young.

Build a fine tomb for my dad.

Michelangelo designed a room where architecture and sculpture fused harmoniously. He drew inspiration from the Old sacristy where the division of space is emphasised by the alternating of whitewashed walls and grey serena stone, but he interpreted it in his own personal way, as only truly great artists are able to do.

Look at the three levels he has divided each wall into. Here they are almost made to contrast with one another: the first is filled with niches, the second is much smoother and the third has a single window.

Michelangelo did not want merely to create an orderly space, but he wanted it to appear animated by internal forces: look for example at the window on the third level, it seems to stretch towards the dome.

The figures he has sculpted seem to possess this same internal vitality. On the right of the entrance look at the tomb of Giuliano duke of Nemours, third son of Lorenzo the Magnificent. Giuliano is shown as a condottiere holding the rod of commander and a coin that suggests his generosity.

Beneath him lie two of Michelangelo's most famous works: Night, a young woman asleep and Day, a strong muscular man but whose face is only roughly hewn.

Opposite is the monument to Lorenzo duke of Urbino, portrayed as a condottiere with armour and helmet.

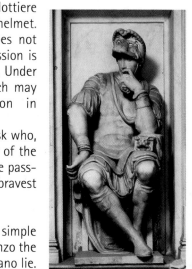

Unlike his cousin though he does not seem ready for action; his expression is serious and absorbed in thought. Under his left arm is a small box which may suggest parsimony (moderation in spending).

Below you can see Dawn and Dusk who, together with the Night and Day of the monument opposite, represent the passing of time, to which even the bravest men have to submit.

To the right of the entrance a simple chest marks the place where Lorenzo the Magnificent and his brother Giuliano lie.

Above there are three statues. Look at the Madonna with child in the middle; the child is shown turning towards his mother to be fed and it is a very tender and affectionate gesture. Michelangelo used a technique called "contrapposto": he arranged the various parts of the body so that they contrasted with one another. Notice how Giuliano's body is straight but his head turns sideways; Lorenzo's body is in the same position but his arms are in a contrasting position; Jesus, turning towards his mother, twists his body round. This makes the sculptures more alive, they seem almost as though they are about to move towards us.

CHAPEL OF THE PRINCES

Go out of the sacristy and go back to the chapel of the Princes, a richly decorated room all covered in precious marbles.

It was commissioned in 1568 by Cosimo I to celebrate the greatness of the Medici family. To build the chapel precious stones and marble were collected all over the world; the long, complicated and costly working of these was the task of the Opificio delle Pietre Dure craftsmen, experts at working semi-precious stones. It took them 300 years! Its magnificence must have astounded whoever went into it. Indeed, although it had been created to house the tombs of the family, the Medici held marriages there, religious celebrations and received the ambassadors of foreign states.

The dome of the Princes' chapel

All around are the tombs of the Medici grand dukes, from Cosimo to Giangastone. There is a gilt bronze statue for each grand duke. The tombs here are honorary monuments though, the real ones are in the crypt.

PIAZZA SAN MARCO

Now go back to via Cavour and, leaving the Medici palace on the left, walk along it until you get to piazza San Marco.

Here in the 13th century a small oratory was built dedicated to St. Mark which in the next century was turned into a large complex of buildings with a church and a monastery, looked after by the Silvestrine monks. These monks were not well loved by the population in their quarter though and so at the beginning of the 15th century the Dominicans from Fiesole tried to take their place. In 1437, thanks to a helping hand by the powerful Cosimo the Elder, they succeeded in their intent.

Cosimo did not merely recommend the Dominicans to the pope but (either as a penitence or perhaps to gain political advantage) he also paid for the San Marco church to be completely restructured. He gave the task to Michelozzo. The large family shields you see almost everywhere are to remind us that for seven years everything was ordered, supplied and paid for by Cosimo's bank. The new monastery was one of the most modern in Italy and in the years that followed many important people stayed there.

Go in at no. 1 in the square and see it.

MONASTERY OF SAN MARCO (SAN MARCO MUSEUM)

The Dominican monasteries were adorned with holy images that accompanied the monks in their meditation and prayer. One of the Dominicans that lived in Fiesole was Friar Guido di Pietro (1400-1455) known because of his kind and generous manner as Beato Angelico. Apart from being a good friar, he was also a clever painter, and so he was charged to carry out the first decorations in the convent.

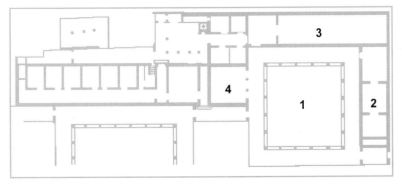

When you go into the **cloister (1)** you will come across an important example of his painting, positioned as if to welcome the visitor. It is a crucifixion with St. Dominic, who you can recognise by his white habit and black cape, typical of his order.

Start going round the cloister. This is where the daily life of the monks took place. It was dedicated to prayer and acts of charity but also to study and work.

On the right of the entrance is the door of the **hospice (2)**, which once served as a refuge for the poor and for pilgrims. Now it is the Beato Angelico museum.

Look for the **Linen makers' tabernacle** of Mary and Child Enthroned, the artist's first certain and dated (1433) work. The precious drapery, woven with gold, envelops the Madonna as if she were in a glass "window". The painting was in fact paid for by the Linen makers, Second-hand dealers and Tailors.

On the opposite wall you can admire the **Deposition from the cross** or **Holy Trinity altarpiece** (1435). In the centre St. John and other saints are supporting the body of Jesus. Next to them is the Madonna with Veronica and the two Marys. On the right Nicodemus is holding the crown of thorns and the three nails that pierced the hands and feet of Christ. Look for a figure with a black hood. It may be a portrait of Michelozzo.

Go out of the hospice towards the **big refectory (3)**, where the community of Dominicans ate while one of them read the Holy Scriptures from the pulpit you see on the right. On the end wall is a large fresco showing the **Crucifixion** (upper part) and the **Providence of the Dominicans** (lower part); look for St. Dominic receiving food from the angels.

Leave the refectory and go to the **chapter room (4)**; here the monks sat on wooden benches around the walls and discussed the most important issues of their community.

On the wall opposite the entrance you can see another fresco by Beato Angelico showing the **crucifixion**: among the many people gathered around the cross, the artist has included St. Dominic and St.Francis, recognisable by his poor brown habit, tonsure (the shaven head typical of the penitent) and golden rays that emanate from his stigmata (wounds like those of the crucified Christ that miraculously came to St. Francis and never healed), as well as numerous other people who did not live at the time of Christ but whom the painter included at Christ's tragic moment.

When you leave the chapter roc a large bronze bell in front of y for the monastery by Cosimo tt It is known as the "whiner", because it is linked to Girolam Savonarola whose followers were called the "whiners"; he became a friar in the monastery and was prior between 1491 and 23 May 1498 when he was put to deatt The "whiner" rang for the las time on 8 April 1498, the day his arrest in the desperat attempt to gather together disciples.

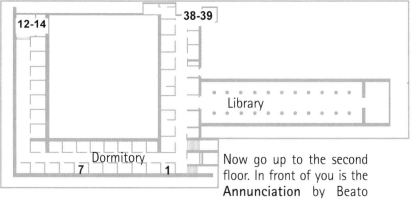

Now go up to the second floor. In front of you is the **Annunciation** by Beato Angelico which seems to greet you as you it greeted the monks when they entered the dormitory. Everything in this painting is harmonious and elegant: the portico with its capitals and the light walls that recall the courtyard below built by Michelozzo, the precious and colourful wings of the angels, the delicate clothes of the Madonna and garden full of flowers. Here the artist used a very expensive mineral called azurite and gold, which you will find only in frescoes that decorate places of particular importance.

The **dormitory** is made up of 39 cells. The cells were the small bedrooms of the monks and contained a straw bed, a kneeler and a small table. Each cell contains a small fresco by Beato Angelico and his assistants, with scenes from the life of Christ. These were to help the monks in their prayers when they woke up and when they went to bed.

Go into **cell 1**. You can see the risen Christ appearing to Magdalen near the empty tomb. Magdalen kneeling, her face covered in tears, raises her face to Jesus who seems to move away saying "Do not touch me".

Look for an item that does not seem to belong to the scene.

Go to **cell 7**, here Christ is being derided and scoffed at before being put to death.

The insults and punishments are represented by symbols. Which?		
1..........................	2.....................	3.............................

At the feet of Jesus are the Madonna and St. Dominic who you can recognise by the book, the white habit and star over his head.

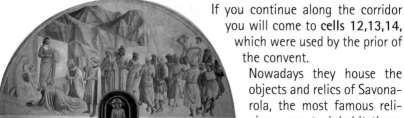

If you continue along the corridor you will come to **cells 12,13,14,** which were used by the prior of the convent.

Nowadays they house the objects and relics of Savonarola, the most famous religious man to inhabit them. At the end of the third corridor are **cells 38, 39** reserved for Cosimo the Elder. These are where he would retire to reflect and meditate. Cell 39 has a fresco showing the Adoration of the Magi.

Where have you seen a fresco of the same subject?
1. in the Medici palace chapel
2. in the new sacristy in san Lorenzo
3. in a grotto in the Boboli gardens

On your way back to the entrance, you will come to the **Library** completed in 1444. It is one of the most beautiful of Michelozzo's creations and one of the most important parts of the monastery because the Dominicans dedicated most of their time, when they were not praying, to studying.

This room contained the precious books that humanist Niccolò Niccoli collected around and about, spending his entire fortune in the meantime. Cosimo bought them and bequeathed them to the Dominican fathers, much to the glorification of his own name.

For the Renaissance man, culture and art had a 'political value'. They helped to demonstrate how great their power was.

PIAZZA SANTISSIMA ANNUNZIATA

When you come out of San Marco, turn left along via Battisti. Continue until you get to piazza Santissima Annunziata. Go into the centre of the square, and with your back to the large bronze sculpture, look at the three loggias that surround it.

This extremely harmonious whole is in actual fact the result of three very clever but different architects who

each worked a hundred years apart!

OSPEDALE DEGLI INNOCENTI

Please leave your babies here

Thank you

From the end of the 13th century there was a large open space in this area which was used for the weekly market of produce coming from the country. In 1419 the Silk Guild decided to build a hospital for abandoned babies here and Filippo Brunelleschi was called to design the building. In the Middle Ages there had been buildings with open loggias, but for the building you see on your right Brunelleschi thought up a new architectural form which followed the rules of the Renaissance style (@ 12). He renewed tradition by creating a modular building, that is one whose proportions are based on the repetition of the same measurement.

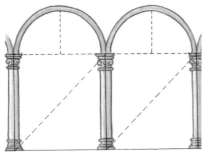

He devised a much lighter portico than those built in the Middle Ages, using slender columns instead of pilasters.

To understand how Brunelleschi's module works try imagining this façade divided into lots of equal squares, with columns whose height is equal to the width of the arches; even inside the

building we find the same harmony in the layout of the rooms.

Another feature of Brunelleschi's art is the alternation of light plaster and dark ribbing that emphasise the rhythm of the building and which we find in many other buildings designed by him. The empty spaces between the arches contain round terracotta sculptures of babies in swaddling clothes. These provide

the only touches of colour and are the work of Andrea della Robbia.

Brunelleschi, did not finish the hospital because at the time he was occupied on the Cathedral dome, but he still kept the work in mind. Some say that he chose this square as one of the best places from which to view Santa Maria del Fiore. The Innocenti hospital is involved in promoting the culture of childhood even today.

LOGGIATO DEI SERVITI

Brunelleschi's hospital started off the renovation of the square. It was such a success that 100 years later the friars of the order of the servants of Mary, who administered the church of the Santissima Annunziata, decided to build a second portico the same as the 15th century one. You can see it opposite the hospital.

CHURCH OF THE SANTISSIMA ANNUNZIATA

Almost another century passed before the façade of the church was given a loggia too. This occurred in 1601.

Originally it had a single small arch above the entrance door where in 1513 Pontormo (1494-1556) painted a fresco of two women (Faith and Charity) either side of the coat of arms of Leo X, the first Medici pope. This influential family is remembered in the square also by the large bronze statue of Ferdinando I, who wished to be portrayed on horseback like his father Cosimo I.

> Where is the statue of Cosimo?
> 1. in piazza San Marco
> 2. in piazza della Signoria
> 3. in piazza Santa Maria Novella

Piazza Santissima Annunziata had a market, religious buildings, a hospital and works of art dedicated to the Medici. This was not unusual in the Middle Ages nor in the Renaissance when religious life and lay life were closely linked. A reminder of this can be found in a feast that is celebrated in the square on the evening between 7 and 8 September, the traditional day of the birth of the Madonna.

Oh, nice Rificolona

The feast is called the **Rificolona** which takes its name from a paper lantern lit with a candle that the Florentines carry in the street on that evening. The feast celebrates the night-time habit of the farmers to go and give thanks to the Madonna of the Santissima Annunziata, using a paper lantern to light their way. If you are in Florence on these days, you take one too, but be careful - the favourite past time during the feast is to bombard other people's lanterns with peashooters!

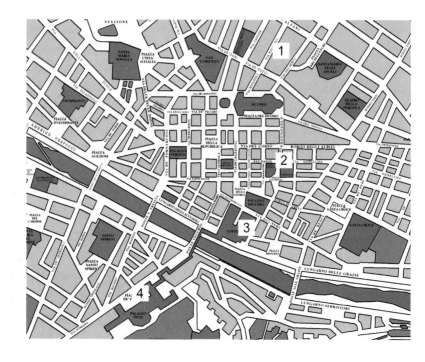

1.   Galleria dell'Accademia
2.   Bargello Museum
3.   Uffizi Gallery
4.   Pitti Palace (Palatine gallery, Silver museum, Boboli gardens)

Galleria dell'Accademia: weekdays 8.30-22; holidays 8.30-20. Closed Monday

Bargello Museum: 8.30-13.50. Closed the 2nd and 4th Monday and 1st and 3rd Sunday of the month

Uffizi Gallery: weekdays 8.30-22; holidays 8.30-20. Closed Mondays

Palatine Gallery; weekdays 8.30-20. Closed Monday

Silver Museum: 8.30-13.50. Closed 1st and 3rd Monday and 2nd and 4th Sunday of the month

THE GREAT MUSEUMS OF FLORENCE

During the Renaissance the rich families of Florence commissioned artists for works no longer only destined to embellish the city but also the rooms of their grand palaces. All the important personages had to have a private collection that would testify to his wealth and love of culture. Many of the objects that we can admire today in the Florentine museums come from these collections.

Between a collection and a museum though there is more than just a name. The collections of the noblemen and the wealthy signori of the Renaissance were made up of countless types of item arranged so as to have the maximum effect on their guests possible: paintings and weapons, jewels and sculptures, silver and so on.

From the end of the 18th century though the idea was born that the beauty of these private collections should be available for everyone to see, and so they were turned into museums open to the public.

The museum was to house the objects, look after them and show them off as clearly as possible. Many collections were reorganised, the items were divided into categories (paintings, sculptures, etc.) and then exhibited in a specific way.

Nowadays the museums of Florence are among the most famous in the world!

GALLERIA DELL'ACCADEMIA

The gallery, which is in the 14th century monastery of San Matteo, was created in 1784 by grand duke Peter Leopold I of Lorraine. He wanted to make it easier for the young who attended the art school of the Academy to study their subject. In

Pietro Leopoldo

those days to become a clever artist it was thought necessary to practise copying masterpieces of the past, in particular those of the Florentine artists. With the passing of time the collection increased so much that now it is one of the largest collections of 14th century painting.

That? Oh my uncle did it!

However, the event that made it famous was the arrival of Michelangelo's David, brought here in 1873 from the piazza della Signoria. Initially in 1910 its place was taken by a copy, sculpted by Luigi Arrighetti, a sculptor from Sesto Fiorentino. This allowed his nephew to say to tourists: "My uncle did that!"

Once you have passed the ticket office you will come to a large corridor entirely dedicated to the works of **Michelangelo Buonarroti** (1475-1564); walking along you can see the four sculptures known as the **Prisons**, or the **Slaves**.
Michelangelo sculpted them in 1530 for the tomb of pope Julius II which was to be adorned with some 40 statues like these! An exceptional feat, which the artist never terminated.

Between the two Prisons on the right you can see **St. Matthew**, begun in 1505 but never finished. Why didn't Michelangelo finish his works?
One explanation is that the artist did not trust anyone to assist him and so he did all the work himself, taking much longer than others and at times getting involved in works that were just too much to carry out. But this is not the only reason.

Now we'll see what they make of this!

According to many experts Michelangelo's "unfinished" works did not need perfecting but were the end result and how the artist wanted them.

In this way he found a convenient way of showing the drama of man, who tries to free himself from his material earthly part (his body) because it oppresses or constrains him.

Following on you come to a group on the right called the **Palestrina Pietà**. Although it is exhibited along with the works of Michelangelo we do not know who it is by.

At the end of the corridor is a work that, unlike the others, the artist managed to complete in just three years, between 1502 and 1504.

It is the **David** commissioned by the Florentine Republic who wanted a work that would symbolise courage and love of freedom.

Other artists had tried unsuccessfully to use a huge block of white Carrara marble that had been lying in the deposits of the Opera del Duomo for a good 35 years.

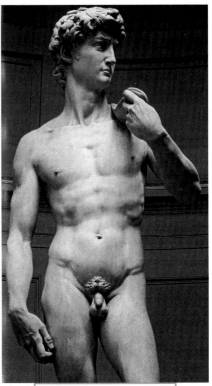

David by Michelangelo

Michelangelo, who was then only 27, was not frightened by the technical difficulties and, sculpting the stone directly there in the deposits, he began to model it.

He did not want to portray a victorious David, captured in the moment when he had already slain the giant Goliath, but instead a young man preparing for the fight, decided and fully aware that the salvation of his people depended on him and his skill.

As the we read in the Bible, David was a humble shepherd who had gone to help his brothers in the war between the people of Israel, led by Saul, and their eternal enemies the Philistines. All of a sudden Goliath came forward from the lines of the Philistines. He was a giant and fearsome warrior who, armed to the teeth, insulted the people of Israel and their God. During the general panic and horror David took up Goliath's challenge. Armed only with a sling, he knocked Goliath to the ground with a stone then cut his head off with the giant's own sword, gaining freedom and victory for the Hebrews.

David slaying Goliath was a theme much loved by Florentine artists, who usually showed him as a much younger boy with boots, sometimes a headdress and with Goliath's head at his feet.

Michelangelo instead shows him as a young and powerful hero, with the athletic body of a classical statue.

Despite the glorious welcome it at once received, the long life of the famous sculpture has not been an easy one.

In 1527, during the fight against the Medici, someone in palazzo Vecchio threw a bench out of the window which broke David's left arm in three places. The pieces of marble stayed on the ground for three days until the young Giorgio Vasari picked them up and had it restored.

In 1544 the left shoulder fell off killing a poor peasant, in the square to pay his respects to Cosimo.

The David was restored again and it then spent three centuries of relative peace.

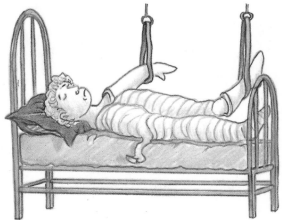

In 1870 though it was noticed that the David was losing its balance and was leaning forwards.
So it was decided to move it to a new site created especially for it, the tribune of the Accademia gallery.

On 30 July 1873 its removal began. It lasted ten days. Finally on 8 August the David arrived at its new home.
But the tribune was not ready and so the statue stayed wrapped up for a long time and the lack of air caused mould spots on the marble.
The people said that David had measles and needed a cure.
The protective wrapping was taken off and hey presto he was cured!

In 1882 the tribune was completed, but the adventures of the statue were not over yet.

A few years ago in 1992 a madman broke one of the feet with a hammer.

Before leaving the gallery you can see what Michelangelo looked like in a portrait to the right of the David.

BARGELLO MUSEUM

This museum is to be found in the large building (@34) that looks like a town castle, right behind piazza della Signoria. It was founded in 1860 and is now one of the most important museums in Italy for Medieval and Renaissance sculpture. Go in and when you have passed the ticket office, you will be in a courtyard with a beautiful well in the centre. The walls and pilasters are adorned with the coats of arms of many of the Podestà and Captains of the People who lived here. When the palace became a prison, the large open arches you see on the ground floor were walled up and filled with cages positioned at various heights. Other cages filled the rooms on the upper floors; it had been made a truly miserable place. People were put to death in this courtyard. The less important prisoners were hanged and the more highly bred ones had their heads cut off.

Go into the room dedicated to the Middle Ages opposite the entrance (1). Look at the three figures in the sculpture in the middle of the wall in front of you; they are **Mary enthroned, with St. Peter and St.**

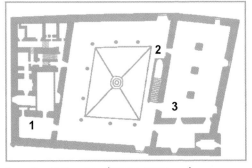

Paul, by Arnolfo di Cambio (1245-1302 ca.)
The artists in the Middle Ages were not interested in showing human figures realistically; here for example, the three figures are all the same height even though Mary is seated. The size of the personages is connected to their importance in the Christian faith! Look at Jesus; the artist not only shows him as bigger than a baby of only a few months but also in the position and with the expression of an adult. He is standing up and looking straight in front of him with a serious look on his face. In one hand he is holding a roll (the shape of ancient books and symbol of divine law), while with the other he is in the act of blessing.

As time passed, this way of representing the human figure changed: look at the **Madonna with baby Jesus** near you on the left. The child Mary is holding in her arms is clearly very young and is playing with a little bird. There is also a slight sense of movement in the body of the Madonna. Although it is not a very natural one, it is still something in comparison with the complete rigidity of the three figures you looked at before.

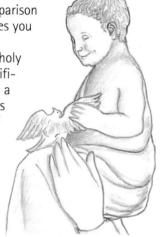

The sculptor lets you know that these are holy figures by including details of religious significance: the lily the Madonna is holding is a symbol of purity and the little bird, with its wings spread open, alludes to the death of Jesus on the cross.

Now go back into the courtyard and go up to the upper loggia **(2)**.

Immediately to the right is the **General Council hall, or Donatello room** where there is a collection of 15th century sculptures.

In the centre of the room on the left, look for a standing figure of a young man dressed in woollen clothes and a cloak. At his feet is a sling and... a head!

It is the statue of **David** sculpted by Donatello between 1408 and 1412, when he was just over twenty. Do you know the story of David and Goliath? (@98).

Donatello is a Renaissance artist and he wants to show all the elements of the scene realistically - the huge head of Goliath with the stone embedded in his forehead, the young man's sling leaning on the head. Just think that to make the scene even more realistic, Donatello added a strip of leather that went from David's right hand to the body of the sling. Yet despite all these innovations the young man still does not move naturally and, like the Madonna you saw before, it seems to lean to one side.

Nearby, in the middle of the end wall there is another work by Donatello: **St. George**, commissioned by the Armour and Sword makers Guild between 1416 and 1420 for the Orsanmichele church (@38). It remained there until the end of the 19th century when it was replaced by a bronze copy and taken to the Bargello. It was sculpted only a few years after the David, yet the artist has learned new techniques. In order to show the soldier-saint's enormous energy he does not have him wavering about - he stands straight, his feet firmly placed on the ground. The simultaneous turning of the bust towards the right and head to the left give the statue a sense of movement. The saint seems almost to have just moved - something has attracted his attention and he turns his lead, just like you would. Imagine if someone called you from behind now, how would you turn?

Finally, between the marble St. George and the David, there is another version of **David**. This one, also by Donatello, is in bronze and was carried out around 1440.

Before starting this work he had made a trip to Rome where he had been profoundly impressed by the classical art he saw there. So, like the classical Greeks and Romans, he created a statue 'in the round', that is to say that stands in its own space and that the observer can walk around and see from all angles.

This was a novelty for the 15th century. Until then sculptures had been used to decorate architecture and their backs were usually in a niche or against a wall. Instead here the sculpture is independent, in its own space, just like in reality.

Another work by Donatello, characterised by this faithful reproduction of reality, is the **Portrait of Nic-colò da Uzzano** in the middle of the room. The idea of the head being turned is repeated here, but this time it is not a holy figure but one of the most powerful men in Florence in the 15th century.

Before you leave, you can have a look at the famous panels showing the **Sacrifice of Isaac** by Lorenzo Ghiberti and Filippo Brunelleschi made for the Baptistery door (@49).

Go down to the ground floor and to your left is the large **Sixteenth century sculpture room,** or **Michelangelo room (3).** Look for the **Drunken Baccus,** sculpted by Michelangelo between 1496 and 1497 during a visit to Rome. In Rome the artist saw a great many works of classical art and these inspired him not only as far as the subjects were concerned (Bacchus was the god of wine and enjoyment), but also in his way of representing them. Notice how the god seems to be unsteady on his bent heavy legs. The small satyr at his feet is in a complex pose too, with his bust twisted round while he eats grapes from the hand of the god.

This room contains other works by Michelangelo. Look on the left for the **Pitti Tondo,** which he carried out at the beginning of the 16th century. This low-relief shows Mary with Jesus, a theme that you have come across many times. The great Michelangelo does not just show the figures realistically and harmoniously though. He places them in a limited and restricted space, yet he manages to make them come alive, using brilliant new solutions.

Notice how Mary's head comes out of the frame of the tondo, as if it were facing towards the outside rather than towards the centre of the composition, and how in certain areas the marble is perfectly smooth and reflects the light, while in others it is just roughly sculpted. You can find this technique called non-finito, unfinished (@97), again in the **Brutus,** made much later by Michelangelo, in 1540.

Here the non-finito is used to give the face a strong expression. This bust may have been inspired by an event that happened in 1537. Lorenzo de' Medici killed his cousin the hated duke Alessandro, just as Brutus had killed Julius Caesar, his adoptive father. Both Alessandro de' Medici and Caesar held the power of their cities in their hands and ruled as despots.

UFFIZI GALLERY

In 1560 Cosimo I de' Medici commissioned architect Giorgio Vasari to design a large palace where all the city's administrative offices (uffizi) could be located. The new construction was built next to palazzo Vecchio where the Medici family then lived and from where it governed Florence.

Right after the ticket office you will come to a portrait of Anna Maria Luisa de' Medici, a very important person for Florence and its museums. She was the last descendent of the family and she bequeathed the Medici collections to the Lorraine family, who were the new lords of the city, on the condition that the collections should stay in Florence. At the end of the 18th century the museum, the first in the world, was opened to the public.

Go to the first floor. Here you can see one of Maria Luisa's ancestors, Francesco I de' Medici. In 1581 he began taking the precious objects that his father Cosimo had kept in a room at the palazzo Vecchio to the Uffizi. Above is a painting of the entrance to the theatre that he had built for court entertainment.

Go up two more flights of stairs. Now you are at the gallery but, before you go in, look up... there is a third person you should meet!. It is Peter Leopold of Lorraine, who at the end of the 18th century reorganised the collection and turned what had been a private collection into a museum.

These corridors, now filled with works of art, were originally open loggias without decoration. In 1581 Francesco I closed them with windows, had the ceilings frescoed and began to move the family collections here. He began with the "illustrious men", a series of portraits of famous personages, all the same size.

They are not the only illustrious ones present though. The most famous exponents of the Medici family can be seen among a group of larger portraits.

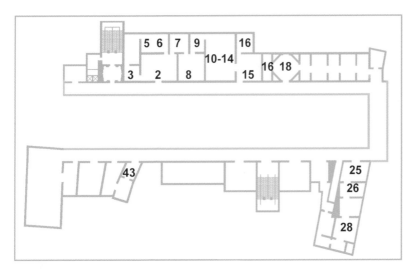

Start your visit in **room 2**. It contains paintings of the 13th and 14th centuries.

Look for the paintings of the Madonna enthroned with baby Jesus in her arms; these are also called **Maestà**, or Majesties, because they show Mary as a queen.

The gold background which seems to envelop the figures represents divine light. Have a look at the painting where Mary is seated on a marble throne. It was painted at the beginning of the 14th century by **Giotto**. He was a great artist who updated the style of painting of the previous century by making the holy figures he portrayed appear much more realistic. Look at Mary, she is shown as a real woman. Her breasts and knees show through her

Maestà by Giotto

clothes, her hair can be seen under her veil and her cheeks and lips are pink. Turn to the painting on the right. It is the work of Giotto's master, **Cimabue** and was painted in around 1280. Unlike his pupil he does not show Mary's body or hair and her face is all the same colour.

On the other side is a third **Maestà**, carried out in 1285 by **Duccio di Buoninsegna**, a painter that came from Siena. He painted with great attention to decorative details and to the alternating of colour, in a style that was to become typical of his city. His way of painting Mary is even less realistic then Cimabue's. The Madonna is completely wrapped up in her veil and although her face

Maestà by Duccio   does turn slightly, it is stylised and distant.

These two artists also showed the throne 'held up' by angels that do not seem to be feeling the weight though!. Mary and Jesus are feather light, as if they were made of pure spirit. In Giotto's painting instead, the throne is set firmly on the ground. Angels and saints crowd about, occupying all the space around and behind.

Looking at the three paintings one after the other and paying careful attention to all these details, you will notice that they represent three different stages in the course of a move towards representing figures in their own space, closer and closer to reality.

Now go into **room 3**, which contains **14th century paintings from Siena**. There are two works that were in Siena Cathedral. Opposite the entrance is the **Annunciation** painted in 1333 by **Simone Martini** and on the opposite wall the **Presentation of Jesus in the Temple** by **Ambrogio Lorenzetti** (1342). Here you find the harmony, elegance and wealth of detail that you saw in the Maestà by Duccio and

Detail of the Annunciation
by Simone Martini

that are features of the painters from Siena. Compare the two paintings. The work of Simone Martini is undoubtedly less realistic. It seems not to take Giotto's innovations into account, but this does not mean that his painting is less beautiful or he less clever; but just that it has been done differently and according to a different taste. The scene takes place in Mary's home, but the artist does not represent the details of her house.

Which of these could he have included to show the interior of a home?

How does Simone Martini show that the angel has just arrived?
1. its cloak has not touched the ground yet?
2. its wings are still open
3. Mary looks rather afraid

What device does he use to show that it is talking to the Madonna?

....

Ambrogio Lorenzetti instead shows Jesus taken to the Temple by his parents. All first-born Hebrew children had to be consecrated to God by the sacrifice of two turtle-doves or, if the family were poor, two ordinary doves. The artist wanted the scene to be realistic, so he painted the many details very carefully.

Try finding:

However, despite all the care over the details, the scene would not have seemed realistic if Ambrogio had not followed Giotto's teachings and used a particular technique that enabled him to create a sense of depth. This is called perspective, and from the 14th century onwards, it was used increasingly by artists to give the idea of some objects being further away than others.

Go towards **rooms 5-6**. Immediately to the left of the entrance you can see the **Adoration of the Magi** painted in 1422 by Lorenzo Monaco, so called because he was a monk of the Camaldolesian order (monaco means monk). In the background on the left is the stable with the ox and the donkey, and in the foreground on the extreme left, Joseph sitting on the ground. Look at Mary with the baby in her arms; the artist shows them higher up than the other figures (so underlining their importance), but as he did not want to put them on a throne (which would have seemed very odd in a poor stable), he sat them on a raised rock.

We don't need it, you donkey!

The Visitation by Gentile da Fabriano

Now on the wall at the end on the right, look for the same subject painted in 1423 by **Gentile da Fabriano** for the Strozzi, a family of rich bankers who commissioned this work for the family chapel in the Santa Trinità church.

Here too the Magi have come to pay homage to Jesus yet, in this case, they seem to be the most important figures! Look at the king in the centre of the scene, dressed in gold brocade, extremely fashionable among the rich gentlemen of the time.

The splendour of the clothes does not have religious significance, but is connected to the fact that the Strozzi traded in fabrics, so painting them so splendid was a way of advertising their activity!

Another symbol of power and wealth is the presence in the painting of monkeys, cheetahs, greyhounds, animals that were bred by the richest families of Florence.

While the painters of the Middle Ages created works that were full of symbols that were instructive to the people, who did not know how to read or write, from Giotto onwards the interest of the artists turns towards nature, animals and man. From this moment on there is an attempt to portray pictures - even religious ones - realistically.

Try connecting the animals to the two different ways of representing them: that of a Medieval painter and of an artist of the 15th century.

Go into **room 7** and look on the right wall for the **St. Lucy Altar-piece**, painted in 1445 by **Domenico Veneziano**.

The painting shows Mary enthroned with four saints at her sides; the Madonna on the throne has been set by the artist in a space enclosed with niches and arches on columns. You have already seen painted architectural space in other works but none so realistic as this. Here it really seems to contain the figures. The artist was able to do this by applying the rules of linear perspective formulated by Brunelleschi.

In the Middle Ages, to show space, they merely made the lines that went into the background converge without taking any notice of where they terminated. Filippo Brunelleschi, working on scientific principles, established a precise rule: all lines converge at a single point, called the "vanishing point".

In Domenico Veneziano's painting the vanishing point is Mary's lap. The things above that line (the vaulting of the loggia) are seen from the bottom, while all the things below (the first two steps of the throne and the floor) are seen from above.

Look for instance at the halos. Up until now artists had shown them as flat gold circles, the same for saints shown in profile as those shown full on; now instead they have become transparent circles of gold shown according to the point of view.

Like space, the figures are shown more realistically too.

Mary is a young woman, her hair is uncovered and she is wearing an elegant dress; St. Francis wears his habit, St. John the Baptist, in his

animal skins, has the tired and thin look of one that lives in the desert; on the other side St. Zanobi wears the clothes of a bishop (he was bishop of Florence) and St. Lucy has a smart pink tunic and a plate on which are laid her eyes, torn out during her martyrdom. There is another innovation too, look at the sky... it is blue, as in reality!

This new interest for reality in the Renaissance leads to a more faithful representation of men, characterised by the portrait.

On the left there is a diptych (a painting composed of two boards) on which **Piero della Francesca** painted **Federico da Montefeltro**, duke of Urbino and his wife **Battista Sforza** in 1465. Federico was a brave condottiere but also a clever politician and he did not only fight in the service of the powerful but also managed to earn himself a territory of his own and

Federico da Montefeltro

Battista Sforza

the title of duke. He was also a great lover of the arts and sciences and wanted to turn his court at Urbino into an important centre of culture, as Lorenzo the Magnificent was doing in Florence.

Federico wished to be portrayed faithfully, so the artist included the bad side of his looks as well - the lines, warts and hooked nose that had come from the blow of a sword. Apparently it was to show off his bad wound that he always liked to be portrayed in profile!

On the left wall look for the **Battle of San Romano**, painted in 1456 by **Paolo Uccello**. This, with two other similar paintings (one in the Louvre museum in Paris now and one in the National Gallery in London), decorated the bedroom of Lorenzo the Magnificent at the Medici palace.

They refer to the great battle fought and won on 1 June 1432 by the Florentines against the Sienese and Visconti of Milan. Paolo Uccello, whom Vasari defined as "sick with perspective", applied the rules as a test of skill. Notice how he varies the size of the figures, or how he crosses the broken lances on the ground to create an impression of depth.

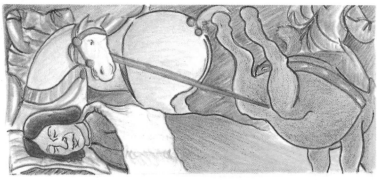

Now go to **room 8** containing works of sacred art by Florentine artists of the 15th century.

Look for the **Madonna with child and angels** by **Filippo Lippi**.

In the painting try to find the elements that characterise the painters of the 15th century and that you have already found in the work by Domenico Veneziano.

Then go to **room 9**. On the wall opposite the entrance you will see some small paintings.

Where were such small paintings kept?
1. in church
2. in niches along the street
3. in the home protected by a case

The first two tables were painted by an artist called Sandro Botticelli (1445-1510). They show the story of Judith and Holofernes.

Giuditta
by Sandro Botticelli

In which famous square can you find these personages?

The other two tell the story of Hercules who, with his strength and cleverness managed to overcome 12 terrible trials. Here he is shown while fighting the Hydra (a many-headed monster) and Antaeus (son of Mother Earth). They were painted by artist named Antonio del Pollaiolo (1431-1498), son of a chicken vendor, famous for its ability to represent the muscles of the human body in movement. Botticelli instead was famous for the elegance of his figures; look at the Judith returning to her city with a light step and a sad expression followed by a handmaid who carries the head of Holofernes. The artist has dealt with a dramatic story but he does not show the most bloody side of it.

Hercules and the Hydra
by Antonio del Pollaiolo

Go to **rooms 10-14** where most of Botticelli's works are exhibited.

Many are inspired by a philosophy known as neo-Platonism, according to which it is necessary to seek a balance between the real side of things and the ideal one.

For example, observe the famous painting **Spring**. Here the artist does not show a real wood, but imagines an ideal one: all the fruit is ripe, none of the flowers are trodden down and no animal disturbs the occupants of the scene!

In the middle of this perfect forest is Venus, goddess of love, and her assistant Cupid; on the right is Zephyr, the west wind that joins Flora, giving life to Spring who scatters feathery light, coloured flowers around her; on the left are the three Graces and Mercury, messenger of the gods, busy keeping away the clouds trying to enter the enchanted forest.

Primavera by Sandro Botticelli

In the same room, look for another famous work by Botticelli: the **Birth of Venus from the waters**.

There are two other figures we have already seen, Zephyr and Spring. How can you recognise them?

Now go to room 15 dedicated to **Leonardo da Vinci** (1452-1519), the great Florentine artist who, unlike Botticelli (who represented the ideal side of things), wanted to show things exactly as they were.

Look for the **Baptism of Christ**. It was painted by Verrocchio (1435-1488), Leonardo's master.

Verrocchio was a great sculptor but like all artists of the period he did not restrict himself to a single medium. The story goes that, after having had Leonardo paint the angel on the left, and seeing his talent outclassed by his young pupil he "never wanted to touch colour again".

Leonardo discovered that in nature things do not have, like in paintings, edges outlined in black and so he began to show them blurred, immersed in the area that surrounds them, less and less clear the further away they get.

This painting was made in around 1474; five years Leonardo later worked, this time alone, on the **Adoration of the Magi** that you see on the same wall. In this unfinished painting, almost entirely without colour, the artist did not want to tell the whole story of the Magi, but to focus his attention on a single scene. In the same way he had observed that outlines appear blurred in space, by studying people he learnt the various gestures and expressions they use according to their state of mind. Leonardo does not paint the serene, ideal faces of Botticelli because he knows that "real" people express joy, fear, pain and wonder in their faces. Observe the figures round the Madonna. They each

show wonder and emotion differently but are represented by the artist so that the composition is harmonious; they almost create a crown around the Madonna and her child.

Adoration of the Magi by Leonardo

Go out into the corridor towards the **Tribune (18)**, the oldest room in the museum, built in 1584 by Francesco I to house the most important pieces of the family collection. The grand duke wanted a space where he would feel at the centre of his own territory but also at the same time at the centre of the world and the universe.

Do you want to know how architect Buontalenti managed to achieve this? He built a room with eight sides (like the Baptistery, the oldest building in the city) and furnished it drawing inspiration from the four elements that make up (so it was thought) the earth and the whole of the universe.

air   fire   earth   water

Francesco I had put classical statues and contemporary paintings in the tribune, and some of them can still be seen now. Try to find the aristocratic mother of the duke, portrayed together with one of Francesco's brothers and other famous personages who left their mark on the history of Florence.

Can you recognise any of them?
1...
2...
3...

Leave the tribune and go to the short wing of the Uffizi, where you will be able to admire a beautiful 'double' view: on the left San Miniato, Forte Belvedere and the ponte Vecchio and on the right palazzo Vecchio and Brunelleschi's dome in the background.

Continue along the last corridor where there are works belonging to the 16th, 17th and 18th centuries.

Go into **room 25** where there is an important work by Italy's most famous artist, **Michelangelo Buonarroti** (1475-1564).

Look for a large painting called the Tondo Doni (from its shape, tondo meaning round and from the name of the wealthy Florentine merchant Angelo Doni who commissioned it). It shows Mary, Joseph, baby Jesus and in the background St. John the Baptist as a child.

Like Leonardo, Michelangelo too studied the reality that surrounded him with greater awareness, but he concentrated more on the anatomy of the figures he represented. He was so interested in studying the human body that he attended dissections of dead bodies to see their structure better.

Because of this he is able to

Tondo Doni by Michelangelo

show men in the most complicated poses both in his paintings and sculptures.

Look at the muscular Mary who, to take her baby, does not turn but has him passed over her shoulder, twisting her body round while her legs....are facing the other direction!

Michelangelo said that the degree of perfection in painting increased " the more it moves towards relief". In fact his figures are strong, they occupy their space almost like statues, the colours are bright, violent, almost blinding, the faces are expressive and decided. He expresses his 'message' clearly through these figures - the Christian world, symbolised by Jesus and his family represents a complete rupture with the pagan world, symbolised by the distant figures of naked men. In the middle, between the two worlds is St. John the Baptist who announced the coming of Christ.

Go to **room 26** dedicated to **Raphael** and Andrea del Sarto. Raphael (1483-1520), much younger than Michelangelo and Leonardo, came into contact with the two artists when he arrived in Florence from Urbino in 1504. He admired their works enormously, yet managed to find his own way of interpreting the lesson of his masters.

Madonna with the goldfinch by Raffaello

Look for the **Madonna with the Goldfinch**. Here you can see how at first Raphael assimilates the teachings of Leonardo; the three figures blend into the background, people and things in the distance seem to disappear on the horizon. Now look at the main figures. Raphael communicates the fact that they are closely bound by affection; Mary has just interrupted her reading to observe the two children and her arms seem to surround them in protection. John, with a smile on his face, holds out the little bird for Jesus to caress. Jesus stretches out his hand towards the goldfinch and looks at his cousin. He leans against his mother like small children do before they have learnt to walk properly. Next to this is another famous painting by Raphael, the **portrait of Leo X**, carried out in 1517.

Notice how cleverly he has shown the book, the bell and rich papal clothes and every detail, even an element which reflects the light. Which is it?

Go up to the painting and look at the fringe on the pope's chair. It has been done using a technique that we will find in the work of another famous painter shortly.

Now on the opposite wall look for the **Madonna of the Harpies** by **Andrea del Sarto** (1486-1530). The strange name comes from the monstrous figures. But where are they?

In this painting the holy figures are arranged according to a solemn scheme, but the artist has still managed to make them closer to the onlooker: notice how Jesus is climbing into the arms of the Madonna and... what are the two little angels up to?

Now go to **room 28** dedicated to **Titian** (1488-1576). Here you will find one of the first Renaissance paintings in which a beautiful naked woman is shown, the **Venus of Urbino**, painted in 1538.

What is new here is the fact that the artist does not represent a goddess of idealised beauty but instead a young woman in her room, waiting patiently to be dressed by her handmaids (the young women that served the noblewomen you see in the background), while a dog sleeps calmly at her feet.

Who is the model of the painting? It may be Eleonora Gonzaga, wife of Francesco Maria della Rovere, portrayed, with her clothes on, in another painting in this room.

Notice the contours of the figures. They are not drawn clearly as Michelangelo drew them, nor blurred like Leonardo's.

Titian stabbed at the painting with his paintbrush, making details seem clearly focused from afar but then, when they are seen close up, they appear as a single patch of colour. Look for instance at the small bunch of flowers in Venus' hand.

From far away the flowers seem to have many distinct petals. But this is not so.

This painting "without drawing", introduced by the Venetian painters of the 16th century, is to inspire artists of the following century from different areas and backgrounds. Among these is **Michelangelo Merisi** called **Caravaggio** (1571-1610).
To find him go to room 43.
Look for a young man with brown curly hair with a wreath of grapes and vine around his head raising a chalice to the onlooker as if inviting them to drink. It is **Bacchus**, the ancient god of wine and wild parties.
Look how many different kinds of fruit there are in the basket before him. It seems as though you could reach

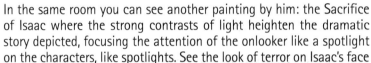

Caravaggio

out and touch them. This effect does not come from the precision of the colour though but from the use of colour.
Caravaggio became very famous because he painted so realistically. He reproduced what he encountered, what he saw, he did not idealise things or make reality less real.

In the same room you can see another painting by him: the Sacrifice of Isaac where the strong contrasts of light heighten the dramatic story depicted, focusing the attention of the onlooker like a spotlight on the characters, like spotlights. See the look of terror on Isaac's face as he realises the nightmare of his imminent death. His body is kept firmly still by his father, his eyes desperately seek help while his screams of terror are almost audible... but the strong and determined hand of the angel holds the father back.

Now you can go towards the exit. On your trip through the centuries you have seen how the way of painting has changed through time, along with the mentality of man.

Bacchus by Caravaggio

PITTI PALACE

Pitti palace in the eighteenth century

You are standing in front of the great Pitti palace which was the residence of the Medici from the 16th century, then that of the Lorraine and, between 1865 and 1871, of the Savoys.

In around 1440 Luca Pitti, a wealthy Florentine banker, then an ally of the Medici, decided to build a grand palace on the Boboli hill. He called Filippo Brunelleschi, the most famous architect of the time, to design it for him. Brunelleschi devised a magnificent building (some say using the project refused by Cosimo for the Medici palace). However work was never terminated because the Pitti family fell into financial ruin, crushed by the success of the Medici.

Over a century later in 1549, Eleonora of Toledo, the wife of Cosimo I, bought the palace. It is said that the noble daughter of the viceroy of Naples did not like the closed dark spaces of the Medieval palazzo Vecchio and wished to live in a place that was full of light and surrounded by green.

So it was that the palace was turned into a splendid residence by architect Ammannati who enlarged it and created an internal courtyard opening onto a magnificent garden, designed like a work of art. In subsequent periods it was further enlarged and embellished.

Now it is the home of several important museums, the Palatine gallery, Modern Art gallery, Silver museum, the royal apartments, Costume gallery and Coach museum.

PALATINE GALLERY

Go up the wide staircase on the right of the main entrance and to the first floor. In the past this was where the reception rooms and winter rooms of the grand dukes were. In 1771 Peter Leopold of Lorraine decided to use these quarters as a picture gallery (where noble families would exhibit their most important pictures), putting in it the many paintings collected by the Medici that had not gone to the Uffizi.

According to the custom of the time the paintings were exhibited together with ornaments including frames, tapestries and pieces of furniture and they lined all the walls. The paintings are still exhibited in the same way, so that the gallery has kept the feel of a prince's picture gallery of the past.

On entering you are immediately in the **statue gallery (1)** which at the time of Cosimo I was a loggia open onto the courtyard and garden.

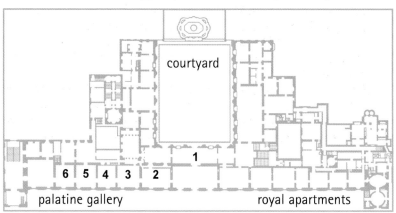

Go towards the **Venus room (2)**, where once the visitors waited before being admitted for an audience with the grand duke. While they waited they undoubtedly looked around them at the luxurious decorations by Pietro da Cortona that narrated the life of the grand duke and his family through mythological figures and symbols. Observe the ceiling: Minerva, the goddess of knowledge chases away a young man from the arms of Venus, goddess of love and takes him to Hercules, god of strength and virtue.

The youth does not seem very pleased but the sacrifice is necessary because, as the Latin motto says, 'the root of virtue is bitter but the fruit is good' (meaning, it is difficult to start being virtuous but the results are worth it). But who is this youth forced to abandon the pleasures of life?

Look at the white figures immediately beneath the ceiling. They are important members of the Medici family in chronological order: the two popes of the family and all the grand dukes right up to the small Cosimo III. That's right, he is the one in the fresco. In order to turn him into a good prince his father wanted him to have a strict upbringing, convinced that it would bring good results.

Go into the **Apollo room (3)** where you will find Cosimo III taking lessons from Apollo, god of the Sun and symbol of knowledge. The god shows him Hercules supporting the weight of the earth, to teach him that the whole world will be his if he has enough virtue.

Next, in the **Mars room (4)**, the prince is involved in battle. You see him while, guided by the light of Mars, god of war, he pierces his enemy with a lance. Do you recognise the coat of arms in the middle of the ceiling? Why is there a crown?

After a great deal of effort and sacrifice the prince eventually is rewarded. On the ceiling of the **Jupiter room (5)**, where the grand dukes seated on their throne received their guests, we find Cosimo III being crowned by Jupiter, king of all the gods.

In the last **Saturn room (6)** here he is again, old now. He is being taken by Mars and Prudence to Saturn, father of the gods (recognisable by his scythe). For his merits the prince is being crowned by Fame (with the trumpet that makes her heard everywhere) and Eternity (who has a circle, the symbol of infinite time).

Fame and glory were reserved for the prince that governed with wisdom and strength. But he had to love art and culture as well. Indeed artists and men of letters of the time were invited to court.

To satisfy their needs the artists tried out ever more sophisticated techniques. Look in this room for the **Madonna of the chair** in which Raphael set to task to organise figures harmoniously within a round space. If you have been to the Uffizi you should remember another painting this shape, the Tondo Doni painted by Michelangelo at the beginning of the 16th

Madonna of the chair

century. While Michelangelo looked for difficult and rather forced poses, Raphael aimed for complete naturalness. Unlike Michelangelo his figures are not in contrast with the shape of the picture, but they adapt to it. Observe the head of Mary, the curved line drawn by Jesus' little foot or his mother's clothes.

Go back into the **Jupiter room (5)** and look on the left opposite you for the **Veiled woman**, another work by Raphael. Here instead of a holy figure, this is the portrait of a woman loved by the painter, the famous Fornarina.

In the **Mars room (4)** there is a work painted a century later, in 1638 by a Dutch painter called Pieter Paul **Rubens** (1577-1640), the **Consequences of war**. Venus, goddess of love, tries in vain to stop Mars, god of war, who is moving threateningly. The god is drawn by Plague and Hunger, terrible and inevitable companions to war. A woman with a broken lute (Harmony that vanishes during periods of war),

another with a child (Love and Life devastated by violence) and a man with the tools of an architect (the Ruin of the city) are crushed by this Fury. On the left is Europe, represented by a woman dressed in black with a tower-shaped

Consequences of war by Rubens

crown. In this painting Rubens seems to be referring to the Thirty Years War, a terrible conflict that afflicted the whole of Europe between 1618 and 1648.

Continuing on your way back, you will come to the **Apollo room (3)** where you will find one of the most famous portraits by **Titian Vercelli** (1488-1576). The subject is a mysterious gentleman known either as the **man with the grey eyes** or the **Englishman**.

Go into the **Venus room (2)** where there are other works by Titian. Look for the portrait of a young woman. It is known as **the Beauty**,
Notice how cleverly Titian has painted her fine dress; the reddish purple of the sleeves, woven with gold thread, contrasts with the varying tones of the heavy midnight blue gold embroidered satin.

The Beauty by Tiziano

Through the slits in the sleeves you can see the thin undershirt which served as underwear. Titian always showed female beauty in all its charm. His paintings were so famous and so sought after that collectors bought them without even knowing who the model was.

Look in the same room for the **portrait of Pietro Aretino** of 1545, in which Titian has portrayed his poet and literary friend. One look tells you that the poet was a brusque man with a strong character who through his poems criticised the hypocrisy and bad behaviour of the 'good society' of his times. He proved himself a harsh observer and his writings were feared by the people that counted.

Well? What have you got to look at?

When he saw the portrait which he was to give to Cosimo I, he said that it had not been completed perhaps because the artist had not been paid enough. Then added that nevertheless the picture " ...breathes, pulsates and moves the spirit as I do in my life".

Go on until you get to the room of the niches (8), the palace's central room, which owes its name to the niches created for classical statues.

ROYAL APARTMENTS

Look how many rooms there are in front of you! The Medici used them as apartments for the first-born son who, under the guidance of the parents, was to be prepared for his difficult role as grand duke. When Peter Leopold created the Palatine picture gallery these rooms became the residence of the grand dukes. The Lorraine family lived here until 1859 and then the Savoys from 1865 to 1871. You can get a taste here of the atmosphere of the princely apartments in which the paintings were simply part of the decoration.

MODERN GALLERY

Go up the main staircase to the third floor. Here you will find the Gallery of Modern Art.
Among the most famous paintings in the Gallery are those by the **Macchiaioli** . This odd name was given to the painters that practised a theory born in France in the middle of the 19th century. They wanted their paintings to represent "the truth as it is and as it seems" and used "blobs of colour and chiaroscuro" which, put close together, gave a very realistic view of the subject.

Rotonda Palmieri by Giovanni Fattori

These artists generally did not paint historical subjects or mythology but events from everyday modern life or landscapes. Look for the **Rotonda Palmieri** by **Giovanni Fattori** (1825-1908). A group of young women are resting in the shade by the sea. Observe the painting carefully. There are no details, yet the scene does not seem incomplete. You will find the same with the **Interior of a cloister** by **Giuseppe Abbati** or **Florentine hills** by **Raffaello Sernesi**.

SILVER MUSEUM

The Silver Museum is in the wing to the left of the entrance where the grand duke's summer apartments were. It was so called because initially the silver items brought back by Ferdinando III from Salzburg were exhibited there. Salzburg was where Federico had been exiled after the arrival in Florence of Napoleon's troops.

In 1923 jewels and precious stones (from the court of the grand dukes) were added to these in 1923 and they are now the main attraction of the museum.

Despite the enormous beauty and immense value of the objects you see, these are only a small part of the treasures of the Medici, most of which was dispersed. Unlike the paintings and sculptures, the Lorraine were not obliged to keep them in Florence.

Once past the entrance you will find yourself in a large frescoed room. Here the people waited in the summer to be presented to the grand duke. It was also used for sumptuous banquets.

The frescoes you see on the walls tell a story: on the left of the entrance an old man with wings and an hour glass beside him, is eat-

ing books! It is Time that consumes everything, implacable enemy of culture and beauty.

In the next scene Satyrs (half man half goat-like creatures), have occupied Mount Parnassus, home of the Muses, protectors of the Arts, and are chasing away Muses, poets and philosophers. Everyone is afraid and is fleeing behind the blind Homer, who in his haste seems to be about to fall! The flight ends at the feet of a woman. It is Tuscany, who indicates a safe refuge, the court of Lorenzo the Magnificent, easily recognisable by his nose and by the winged child bringing him a ring with feathers - his personal coat of arms.

The next scene shows Prudence advising him to bring peace to Italy. This he will do by forcing Mars god of war to put his sword back in its sheath.

Go through the door under this scene. This room, which was originally part of the rooms of the grand duchess, now contains the stone vases collected by Lorenzo. They are very old, most of them Roman.

Which parts of these vases are Renaissance?
1. the handles
2. the parts in metal
3. the lids

Lorenzo had his initials engraved on the stone (LAVR MED, i.e. Laurentius Medici). It proved a good move because it made it possible to recover some of the vases that had been stolen during the siege of the Medici palace just two years after Lorenzo's death in 1494.

Now go back to the large room where the pictures on the walls tell of Lorenzo's love for art and culture. His friendship with great artists and philosophers gains him such merit that after his death his image does not fall in the river Lethe, that consigns everything to oblivion, but is saved by a white swan so that his fame becomes eternal.

Passing the private chapel (it was very small but a lot of people could attend the mass through the small windows) you get to the **Audience hall** where the grand duke received people.

As you can see from the decoration of this room and the previous one, Ferdinando II paid homage to Lorenzo, but his taste was very different. While Lorenzo loved the simplicity typical of the Florentine art of the 15th century, the grand duke preferred more elaborate works.

The object you see in the centre of the room is typical of this new taste at court. It is a cabinet, a valuable piece of furniture which served only to contain the jewels and small items collected by the grand duke. It is made of ebony (a very hard wood, very difficult to work), precious metals and semi-precious stones, the same stones of the classical vases collected by Lorenzo.

 One of the most common forms of courtesy between the various courts was an exchange of gifts. This allowed you to pay homage to your allies and , at the same time, show them how wealthy you were and what excellent taste you had.
This cabinet was a "court gift" from the archduke of Tyrol to Ferdinando II.
This love for precious objects affected even items used for prayer.
Look for example between the two windows at the kneeler of Maria Maddalena of Austria, wife of Cosimo II.

Now turn to the right into the **room of the Semi-precious stones** which contains vases and other items collected by the Medici from the middle of the 16th century. Again you find the love for wealth and grandeur. Every object is embellished with fantastic figures that at times overlap, and various different materials are mixed together to create extraordinary effects. On the left is the **Amber room**. Nowadays we know that amber is a vegetable resin that hardens through time, but at the time the grand dukes thought it originated in the water, which is why the cupboard containing the amber is full of references to the sea world.

From here you can go up to the **mezzanine**. On the left are a number of rooms with exotic items and the silver collection brought from Salzburg, while on the right in two small rooms is what remains of the jewel collection. In the second you will find engraved stones and pearls with irregular shapes, called blister pearls. Their irregularity was the joy of the princes who used them to create strange-looking jewels. The taste of the court never ceases to amaze: look in one of the glass cabinets on the left for a cherry stone with heads engraved on it...!

BOBOLI GARDENS

The Medici's new title meant that a large garden was considered necessary behind the Pitti palace. A new type of park was created, later called an "Italian garden", where the green areas are designed by an architect to form regular shapes and these are filled with magnificent works of art. Go to the back of the palace. Then walk towards the highest point of the garden.

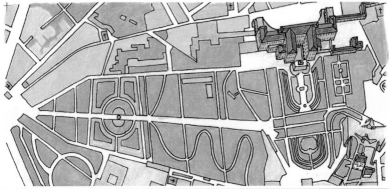

Along the road you will find things listed but they are not in order! Put them in order and mark them on the map. A row of 3 Roman statues including an emperor (with his head covered and the small dish used for ceremonies). 1 big Neptune trying to catch a fish with his trident. 1 statue of Abundance with sheaves of corn and a cornucopia full of good things. 1 large ancient obelisk (1500 B.C.) with a golden sphere at the top.

When you get to the top, go to the left and down the steps to the right and when you get to a fork, take the road on the left, walking alongside some buildings that were originally used by the servants. When you get to the **bird-catcher's lawn** (once this area was used for hunting, one of the court's favourite past times)turn left along a long road flanked by large cypress trees and many sculptures; the last of them include some characters playing blindfold: on the right a boy is trying to hit a crockery pot, on the left others are trying to hit each other... on the head! At the end of the avenue is the **Isolotto square** with the large Ocean fountain.

Turn left. Hey, there's someone in the water! It is the ancient hero Perseus in the act of trying to save Andromeda, who is threatened by a sea monster. Turn round and go up a small avenue. At the end you will come across a man emptying a bucket of newly crushed grape must. Turn right along an avenue that will take you back to your point of departure. On your way to the exit look for: a decorated grotto called the **grotto of Buontalenti** (the architect who designed it) and Morgante the dwarf, one of Cosimo I's jesters whom the prince wanted portrayed mounted... on a tortoise!

USEFUL INFORMATION

The area code for Florence is 055

For tourist information
APT,   piazza Stazione, tel. 212245
          via Cavour 1/r, tel. 290832, 2909833
          borgo Santa Croce 29/r, tel. 2340444

State Museums
Entrance is free up to the age of 18

Medici chapels
Piazza Madonna degli Aldini, tel. 2388602
Opening hours: weekdays 8.30-17, holidays 8.30-13.50. Closed Mondays. Open the first, third and fifth Sunday and second and fourth Monday of the month from 8.30-13.50.

Gallery of Modern Art
Piazza Pitti, tel. 2388616
Opening hours: 8.30-13-50. Closed Mondays.
Open the first, third and fifth Sunday and second and fourth Monday of the month from 8.30-13-50.

Uffizi Gallery
Piazzale degli Uffizi 6, tel. 23885, bookings tel. 2347941.
Opening hours: weekdays 8.30-22, holidays 8.30-20. Closed Mondays.

Galleria dell'Accademia
Via Ricasoli 60, tel. 2388609
Opening hours 8.30-22, holidays 8.30-20. Closed Mondays.

Galleria Palatina
Piazza Pitti, tel. 2388614
Opening hours: weekdays 8.30-22, holidays 8.30-20. Closed Mondays.

Archaeological Museum
Via della Colonna 38, tel. 23575
Opening hours: weekdays 9-14, holidays 9-13. Closed Mondays.
Open the second and fourth Sunday of the month and Mondays following Sunday closing..

Silver Museum
Piazza Pitti, tel. 2388710

Opening hours: 8.30- 13.50. Closed Mondays. Open the first, third and fifth Sunday and second and fourth Monday of the month from 8.30- 13.50.

Bargello Museum
Via del Proconsolo 4, tel. 2388606
Opening hours: 8.30-13.50. Closed Mondays. Open the second and fourth Sunday and the first, third and fifth Monday of the month.

Opificio delle Pietre Dure Museum
Via degli Alfani 78, tel. 265111
Opening hours: from Monday to Wednesday 9-14, from Thursday to Saturday 9-19.
Sundays and holidays closed.

San Marco Museum
Piazza San Marco 1, tel. 2388608
Opening times: 8.30-13.50. Closed Mondays. Open the second and fourth Sunday and the first, third and fifth Monday of the month.

Municipal museums
Entrance is free up to the age of 12

Cenacolo di Santo Spirito
Piazza Santo Spirito, tel. 287043
Opening hours: weekdays 9-14, holidays 8-13. Closed Mondays

Bardini Museum
Piazza de' Mozzi 1, tel. 2342427
Opening hours: weekdays 9-14 , holidays 8-13. Closed Wednesdays.

Santa Maria Novella Museum
Piazza Santa Maria Novella, tel. 282187
Opening hours: weekdays 9-14, holidays 8-13. Closed Fridays.

"Firenze com'era" Museum (Florence as it was in the past)
Via dell'Oriuolo 24, tel. 2616545
Opening hours: weekdays 9-14, holidays 8-13. Closed Thursdays.

Palazzo Vecchio
Piazza Signoria, tel. 278465
Opening hours: weekdays 9-19, holidays 8-13. Closed Thursdays.

Other Museums

Cathedral bell tower
Piazza Duomo, tel. 2302885
Opening hours: summer 9-18.50, winter 9-16.20.

Brancacci Chapel
Piazza del Carmine, tel. 2382195
Opening hours: weekdays 10-17, holidays 13-17. Closed Tuesdays.

Magi Chapel
Via Cavour 1, tel. 2760340
Opening hours: weekdays 9-13, 15-18, holidays 9-13. Closed Wednesdays.

Galleria dell'Ospedale degli Innocenti
Piazza Santissima Annunziata 12, tel. 2491708
Opening hours: 8.30- 14. Closed Wednesdays.

Opera di Santa Croce Museum
Piazza Santa Croce 16, tel. 244619
Opening hours: summer 10-12.30 / 14.30-18.30
Winter 10-12.30 /14.30-18.30. Closed Wednesdays.

Opera del Duomo Museum
Piazza Duomo 9, tel. 2302885
Opening hours: summer 9-18.50, winter 9-18.20. Closed Sundays.

Educational programmes in the museums

Education section of the Soprintendenza ai beni Artistici e Storici
Via della Ninna 5, tel.
Theme-based visits for schools in the state museums, in the Opificio delle Pietre Dure and Horne museum. Free of charge. Bookings should be made at the beginning of the school year.
For teachers: slides and educational material can be loaned, refresher courses organised.

Educational section of Soprintendenza ai Beni Archeologici della Toscana
Via della Pergola 65, tel
Guided visits for schools. Bookings should be made at the National Archaeological museum. Visits are free until Soprintendenza funds run out.
For teachers: information sheets, slides and videos about the museum, Roman Florence and archaeological sites in Tuscany can be loaned.

Education centre for Municipality of Florence area
c/o Ufficio Cultura of the Comune di Firenze
via Ghibellina 30, tel. 2625943
The centre holds courses for teachers wishing to take their students to visit the town's museums. The initiative includes the major municipal museums (Bardini museum, Santa Maria Novella museum, Palazzo Vecchio, Firenze com'era museum), the Archaeological museum, Stibbert museum, Geology and Palaeontology museum, the "La Specola" zoological museum and the Marini museum. Courses, teaching materials and entrance to the museums are free of charge. Bookings should be made by telephone at the beginning of the school year. Further information on the Municipality's education projects can be found in the magazine "Le chiavi della città", sent to all schools in September.

Friends of Florence's museums
Via degli Alfani 39, tel. 289807
Free guided visits for schools to the major museums and places of interest in Florence, class lessons and talks.
A full list of the association's activities can be found in the programme sent to schools at the start of the school year. It is also available from the Secretary.

University museums

Museum of Anthropology and Ethnology
Via del Proconsolo 12, tel. 2396449
Opening times: Thursday to Saturday 9-13.
No entrance charge.
For guided visits call the Friends of Florence's Museums.

Museum of Geology and Palaeontology
Via la Pira 4, tel. 2757536
Opening hours: Tuesday to Saturday 9-13.
Entrance charge: £ 5.000, reduced £ 2.500, school groups £ 10000.
Guided visits for all schools including kindergartens (max. 30 children), cost £ 50.000, entrance fee included.
Telephone bookings

Museum of Minerals and Lithology
Via la Pira 4, teol. 216936, 2757537
Opening hours: Monday to Friday (some Sundays) 9-13.
No entrance charge on weekdays; Sundays £ 5.000, reduced £ 2.500.
Guided visits for schools from elementary onwards (max. 25 children), £ 50.000, entrance fee not included.
Telephone bookings.

History of Science Museum
Piazza dei Giudici 1, tel. 2398876
Opening hours: Monday to Saturday 9.30-13, Monday, Wednesday and Friday 9.39-13 /14-17.
Entrance: £ 10.000, reduced £ 5.000, groups £ 7.500
Guided visits for schools. Telephone bookings Tuesdays and Thursdays tel. 293493. Choice of two itineraries:
1 complete visit of museum, with different routes to suit age groups (max. 25 people), cost £ 110.000, entrance fee not included.
2 lesson at the museum's Planetarium (seven different topics for classes from 5th elementary to secondary schools) for groups (max. 40 people). Lessons from Monday to Saturday, cost £ 130.000, entrance fee not included.

"La Specola" Zoological Museum
Via Romana 17, tel. 2288251
Opening hours: Monday to Saturday 9-12, Sunday 9-13.
Entrance: £ 6.000, reduced £ 3.000.
Guided visits for schools, from elementary onwards (max. 10 children), telephone bookings, cost £ 80.000, entrance fee not included.

"Giardino dei Semplici" Botanical gardens
Via Micheli 3, tel. 2757402
Opening hours: Monday to Friday 9-12, 14.30-17; Wednesday 9-12. No entrance charge
Guided visits for schools from 3rd elementary onwards. Telephone bookings at beginning of school year, free of charge.

SOLUTION TO GAMES

p. 34   Shape - Same (it is a parallelepiped)
Materials - Same (forte stone and marble)
Position of tower - Different (it is to the side of the Bargello)
Type of projections - Different (they are wooden on the Bargello).

p. 35   Dante's beloved is n.3 Beatrice

p. 39   First riddle: St. Mark, the coat of arms is that of the Linen makers and Second hand dealers (south side, via Lamberti); second riddle: St. John the Baptist, Calimala Guild (east side via dei Calzaioli;
third riddle: Four Crowned saints, Stone and Wood masters' Guild (north side, via Orsanmichele);
fourth riddle: St. Eligius, Blacksmiths' Guild (west side, via Arte della Lana).

p. 43   1-C; 2-A; 3-B

p. 48   The coat of arms of the Calimala Guild: an eagle with a bale of cloth in its talons is above the door of the Cross, on the north side (via Cavour).

p. 49   1. true; 2. true; 3. true 4. false.

p. 54   The right answer is n.3

p. 57   The right order is 2. Birth; 1. Visitation; 3. Baptism;
The odd one out is n.4. the multiplication of the loaves and fishes.

p. 58   Not in the fresco are: crutches, plant, washing machine, lamp, clothes hanger.
The person represented in the fresco is Dante.
1-C (St. Peter - keys), 2-D (St. Thomas - holy books); 3-B (St. George - sword and dragon); 4-A(St. Catherine - the wheel);5 -E (St. Paul - sword and book).

p. 60   The son of Lucrezia Tornabuoni was Lorenzo the Magnificent.

p. 62   Crying on the tomb of Michelangelo are: 3 painting, sculpture and architecture.

p. 63   Apart from the cat that does not appear on the monument all the elements listed were taken from the classical world.

p. 64   You can see the grumpy young friar behind St. Joseph.

p. 68   From the square you cannot see: the pyramid, the Pantheon of Rome, the tower of Pisa, the turreted castle.

p. 71   The phrase refers to: 2. A person who judges others but behaves badly himself.

p. 89   1. A soldier spitting as a sign of disgust;
2. The hands hitting him;
3. A hand with a cane beating him.

p. 90   The fresco is 1. In the Magi chapel in the Medici palace.

p. 93   The statue of Cosimo is n.2. In piazza della Signoria

p. 106   The artist could have added the bed and the bench.

p. 107. All three answers are right. To show that the angel is sp
king he paints words that seem to come from its mouth.
The knife is in the priest's left hand; the first woman on
the left wears the earrings; the red book and fire are on
the altar; the gold chain is part of the priest's clothing.

p. 108   The Medieval painter (bottom left) could have painted the
dog, the horse and the fish in a style similar to that of the
three animals at the top of the drawing. The Renaissance
painter instead would have painted them with greater rea-
lism like those in the centre and at the bottom.

p. 111   3. In houses protected in cases. Judith with the head of
Holofernes appears in a copy of the statue by Donatello in
piazza della Signoria.

p. 112   As in the previous painting Zephyr the wind flies lightly fil-
ling his cheeks and letting out a breeze while the dress and
cloak of the figure by some considered to be Spring are
covered with flowers.

p. 114   Easily noticeable are: Lorenzo the Magnificent; Cosimo the
Elder; Eleonora of Toledo and her son and Cosimo I.

p. 115   The knob of pope Leo X's chair.

p. 116   They are in the plinth that supports the holy group.

p. 120   The coat of arms is that of the Medici family.
The crown indicates the noble title of grand duke.

p. 125   The right answer is n.2. the original parts made of metal
were melted down and re-used (something that cannot be
done with stone). You can tell which are the added parts
because they often contain the red Medici balls.

p. 127   The order of the sculptures is: obelisk, Roman statue, Neptune, Abundance.

BIET CHABAD
055-22-474

Printed in May 1999 by
Arti Grafiche Fratelli Palombi
via dei Gracchi 183, 00192 - Rome (Italy)